2001

Meeting God In Quiet Places

F. LaGard Smith

Illustrated by Glenda Rae

HARVEST HOUSE PUBLISHERS
Eugene, Oregon 97402

Cover by Garborg Design Works, Minneapolis, Minnesota

MEETING GOD IN QUIET PLACES
Copyright © 1992 by F. LaGard Smith
Published by Harvest House Publishers
Eugene, Oregon 97402

Library of Congress Cataloging-in-Publication Data

Smith, F. LaGard (Frank LaGard). 1944–
 Meeting God in quiet places / F. LaGard Smith.
  p. cm.
 ISBN-13: 978-0-7369-0189-5
 ISBN-10: 0-7369-0189-2
 1. Meditations. I. Title.
BV4832.2.S5475   1992
242—dc20   92-9176
                                  CIP

Printed in the United States of America
 07 08 09 10 11 12 13 14 15 / BP / 14 13 12 11 10 9 8 7 6 5 4

Dedication

Dedicated to the people
of Buckland, who have
opened their hearts and
homes to make me feel a
part of the village.

And especially to
Jean, the neighbor
one dreams of having
next door.

Appreciation

Some books
are easier to write than others.
This book was transformed
from weakness into strength,
not of my own efforts,
but through the hearts and minds
of Eileen Mason and Betty Fletcher.
They were more than editors,
concerned about form and content.
They taught me to think devotionally,
and to appreciate as never before
the words of the Hebrew writer,
urging us to fix our eyes on Jesus,
the author and "*editor*"
of our faith.

Contents

Foreword

Those of us who are accustomed to reading LaGard Smith know what to expect when we pick up a LaGard Smith book. We expect analytical dissection of difficult controversy. We expect clear-headed, even-balanced discussion of tough questions.

He helped us understand the New Age movement in *Out on a Broken Limb*. He dared wrestle with feminism and the biblical role of women in *What Most Women Want*. His pen became a sword as he battled the battle against abortion in *When Choice Becomes God*.

These works have taught us what to expect from LaGard's writings. We haven't always agreed with him—but we have always been prompted by him. LaGard speaks crisply to the thinking reader and challenges the discerning leader.

That's what you'd expect from a law professor. That's what you'd expect from a seasoned student of the court. That's what you'd expect from an ex-district attorney. Gentlemanly argumentation and clarification. That's what we've grown to expect from LaGard.

This book, however, is not what you'd expect. *Meeting God in Quiet Places* is a book for your heart. This work will introduce you to the other side of my friend LaGard. In these pages, you'll see the soul of a tender, generous servant whose one aim in life is to please his Father.

LaGard has invited us to walk with him through the countryside of England. But as you walk you will see much more than bunnies and sheep. You will see truths of Scripture come alive and the promise of God renewed with each sunrise.

If you are wanting LaGard to guide you into the courtroom debate of heated controversy, you've got the right author, for no one can do it better. But you've got the wrong book. This work carries you not into controversy but into comfort—into the presence of God.

You'll be glad you made the journey.

—*Max Lucado*

The Journey Begins...

"Do two walk together
unless they have agreed
to do so?"

Amos 3:3

In Quiet Places

Schedules. Commitments. So much to do, so little time. Have you ever wanted to escape the pressures of the fast lane? Have you ever thought how wonderful it would be if you could get away and spend time in solitude and contemplation—to truly stop and smell the roses? Are there times when you want to know more about yourself and your purpose for living?

If so, imagine walking through the English countryside, amid quiet villages, grazing sheep, and tranquil hills, where the ordinary cares of life gently give way to fresh perspectives and life-sustaining spiritual insights. Imagine a time of personal reflection in which you not only experience the harmony and beauty of nature, but also search out the heart and mind of nature's Creator and come to know him in a deeper way.

For six months each year I too live in the fast lane. As Scholar in Residence for Christian Studies at Lipscomb University in Nashville, Tennessee, I am immersed in academia. Trying to keep pace with eager students ready to question and challenge every word I say is exhausting in itself. Add to that a grueling travel schedule, and I find myself physically and emotionally drained—longing for an oasis of calm and spiritual renewal.

For the other six months of each year, I leave the classroom and travel to England to write. There I retreat to a cozy cottage in the Cotswolds, about two hours northwest of London. The Cotswolds—meaning "sheep hills"—are aptly named. Five hundred years ago great flocks of sheep roamed the Cotswold Hills. Nowadays there are fewer sheep, but they continue to provide a peaceful touch to the rolling landscape.

Between Shakespeare's Stratford-Upon-Avon to the north and the university town of Oxford to the south, the Cotswolds are graced by several dozen charming villages. Even their names hint of pleasurable hours spent in antique stores and little tea shops serving scones and clotted cream: Bibury, Burford, Moreton-in-the-Marsh, Stow-on-the-Wold, Bourton-on-the-Water.

My own village of Buckland, in Gloucestershire, just south of better-known Broadway, is a gentle scattering of two dozen honey-colored stone cottages along a single lane leading up into the hills. In the middle of the village is a twelfth-century church and a stonework manor house, which is now a luxury hotel. There are no pubs or woolen shops in Buckland—just hardworking, friendly villagers who put out the welcome mat to all who pass by. Nothing could be more typical than Mrs. Knight's little sign on the gate to her garden: "Tea, 25p for church fund." Village visitors sit around neat white lawn tables, leisurely sip their tea, and admire the deep purple hollyhocks at the top of Mrs. Knight's country garden.

That's how it is in Buckland. Unless you just insist on it, there's no need to hurry. Time doesn't exactly stand still here, but it comes close—especially for me. In America, every minute of every day is scheduled months in advance. Over here, except for Sunday, I can forget what day of the week it is and it doesn't matter.

Going to work is even a pleasure. It's as simple as commuting from upstairs to downstairs! And once I'm at my desk, I look out onto fluttering birds on the bird feeder in the apple tree, horses and their riders cantering down the equestrian trail, and villagers walking their dogs up the village lane. Over the hedge and beyond the adjacent field, I have a magnificent view of the hills with their flocks of woolly creatures!

My daily walks on the paths around Buckland have become a never-ending source of strength and renewal. These are quiet times—precious moments of reflection and introspection. These are times when I slow down to appreciate a world I too often ignore—whether the grandeur of a lingering sunset blazing on a distant horizon, or a delicate buttercup at my feet, begging to be picked.

In the pages to come, I invite you to walk with me along these paths and discover for yourself the wonders of the English countryside. Around the villages and in the hills, there is beauty for the eye and nourishment for the soul. Glenda Rae's marvelous pencil sketches capture with warmth, softness, and intimacy the many scenes that have become part of these daily moments with God.

But it's not just nature or village life that we will see on our walks. Every scene presents us with a parable that is rich in spiritual significance. Where nature graces the eye, the God of nature feeds the soul. All around us every day are signs pointing to God—limitless invitations to explore the mysteries of our existence, and precious gifts of love from the One who has made us.

For me, walking in the hills provides the framework for a divine friendship. Though I walk in solitude, I am never alone. God is my constant companion—guiding here, teaching there, but most of all sharing the wonders of life, as would a father walking hand in hand with his child.

The Scriptures tell us that Enoch "walked with God," as also did Noah. It's the way of the righteous to walk each day with God. As the prophet Micah saw it, walking with God leads us to the very heart of our purpose for living: "He has showed you, O man, what is good. And what does the Lord require of you? To act justly and to love mercy and to *walk humbly with your God*." How could we not be humble, knowing that our Maker has invited us to share each day with him, whether we are literally taking a walk or perhaps unable to walk at all?

I appreciate that daily walks, whether literally taken along some path or whether thought of in a more spiritual vein, are easier for some people than for others. If you are like many people, you may have two or three children filling every minute of your busy day; or have to endure that bumper-to-bumper commute across the city every morning and afternoon; or have a job that leaves you so exhausted that taking a walk is the last thing you think of when you finally get home. Whatever your circumstances, you more than anyone know just how precious your quiet times can be. Hopefully these devotionals can compensate for some of the many demands which rob you of those special moments alone.

Of course, reading the pages of this book won't be quite the same as putting on your boots and heading up into the hills. That may have to wait until you can discover the Cotswolds for yourself. But it is my hope that you will enjoy at least some of the incomparable beauty of the English countryside, and— more importantly—experience new depths of love and new heights of faith in your own daily walk with God.

Chapter One

"Those who live in
accordance with the
Spirit have their minds
set on what the Spirit
desires."

ROMANS 8:5

Rabbits

Quietly nibbling. Hopping gingerly here and there. Running flat-out across open terrain. The rabbits in the hills—scores of them everywhere you look—live up to their billing as being one of the most watchable species in the wild. And even though they belong to the rodent family, they're lovable and huggable—or would be, if you could ever get close enough to cuddle one of them in your arms.

Field rabbits aren't a domesticated breed, like tame pet-store rabbits. In fact, in the hills the rabbits take off at the slightest hint of danger. Sometimes all you see are their white tails weaving and bobbing, as if dodging bullets.

What amazes me about the rabbits is that from 200 yards away, often before I have even noticed them, they are already running lickety-split to the safety of their burrows or to the nearest convenient hedgerow. How do they know I'm approaching? It's those ears, right? So much like antennas that we even name television antennas "rabbit ears." But what is it that they actually hear? If you and I had ears of proportionate size to rabbits, would we hear what they hear, or only what we normally hear, except more loudly?

It's not just the size of the ears. Dogs hear distant sounds long before we humans do, and the smallness or largeness of their ears doesn't seem to matter. Surely it's pitch and frequency that make the difference. Animals are simply on a different wavelength. If we humans are listening to an "AM channel," dogs and rabbits are listening to FM stereo! Sometimes I envy the rabbits for their sense of hearing. To be able to tune in to another frequency on the dial of nature would be mind-boggling. Just imagine the sounds we might hear!

But there is already a sense in which I *can* tune in to another frequency. Jesus hinted as much when he repeatedly said to his audiences, "He who has ears, let him hear." *Everybody* has ears. Why would Jesus suggest that we need ears to hear unless he was suggesting that hearing is a matter of tuning in to the *right* frequency—having the *right* ears!

It's one thing to *hear*, and another altogether to *listen*. A husband may hear his wife asking him a question, but is he really *listening*? Is he attentive, concerned, or interested? Sometimes we get so focused on whatever we're thinking about that we don't even notice when someone is speaking directly to us. Our ears are open, but our minds are closed.

Surely that explains why Jesus often taught in parables, those simple stories with spiritual applications which almost anyone can understand—*if he cares to*. Those who don't care invariably miss the point! It's not their ears or their ability to hear that are defective—only their willingness to *listen* to what they hear. Jesus taught in simple parables to test people's *hearts*, not their *ears*.

Perhaps that explains how two people can look at the same universe around them, with one seeing the wonders of an intelligent divine creation and the other seeing nothing but interesting by-products of blind chance. After all, nature itself is the ultimate parable, from which all other parables are taken. Therefore a person whose heart is already turned toward God will easily see God in nature. A person whose heart adamantly rejects God will never find God either in what he sees or in what he hears.

Ironically, the very people whom Jesus accused of not hearing his message were some of the most religious people of his day. In fact, they were often the community's religious leaders. Is it possible that I myself might be "hearing" God while going through the motions of some familiar worship ritual, but not really listening to what he wants me *to be*? Do I know all the right words but nothing of their true meaning? Is my hearing of God more form than substance?

It's true that God has things for us to do by way of worship, but isn't one of the reasons we spend time in his presence to deepen our love relationship with him on a personal level? What we *do* for him is meant to nurture who we *are* in him. So how do we move from merely *doing* to actually *being*?

Imagine, for a moment, that you are sitting alone in a room, quietly reading a book. There are no sounds in the room except the occasional turning of a page, or perhaps a clock ticking away in the background. Do you hear the orchestra playing? It's playing right in your room. Do you hear someone telling about today's news events? It's happening right in your room. All of this and more is happening in the quietness of your room, if only you want to listen to it. All you have to do is flip a switch. If you have a radio or television, those electronic sound waves are in the room with you right now!

In much the same way, there is also a spiritual dimension which surrounds and permeates our material world. Think of it as the realm in which angels exist—and Satan. It is in this unseen world that the Holy Spirit moves and in which spiritual warfare is taking place. The spiritual dimension is the arena of prayers and miracles. It's the world of the supernatural, the transcendent—a trysting place between the human and the divine.

Unfortunately, getting in touch with the spiritual dimension is not always as easy as flipping a switch. In fact, sometimes tuning in to it can be difficult. Our own spirits are meant to be the receivers which put us on the right wavelength with God, but often our hearts and minds are full of static!

The most serious barrier to our quest for true spirituality is a constant jamming of the frequencies. Just as radio and television transmissions can be jammed in such a way that no one can tune in to them, our desire to hear God can also be drowned out by interference.

How can we listen to God when we can't even hear ourselves think? Both the incessant noise and the daily distractions of a high-intensity society tend to jam any hope we might have of hearing that "still, small voice" of God. In order to tune in to God, we may have to tune out the television and anything else that diverts our attention.

Rabbits have also taught me something else: the critical importance of using my ability to hear. For rabbits, hearing is an early warning system. Their lives literally depend upon their hearing the approach of danger. How then should I expect to know when I am in spiritual danger unless I have my heart tuned to a God who warns me, through his written revelation, of the many threats to my spiritual well-being? Being spiritually hard of hearing could one day prove to be disastrous.

I love watching the rabbits on the hill. But I think they must be there for more than my amusement. If the rabbits on the hill can teach me anything, maybe it's that I need to make sure I'm on the right wavelength: God's wavelength. As one who has been given ears to hear and a heart to understand, I need to tune in more and more each day to the spiritual dimension around me, and then listen like I've never listened before!

Chapter Two

"Trust in the
Lord with all
your heart."

PROVERBS 3:5

Balloons

There they are—toys for grown-ups! Always somewhat fanciful, a bit like cotton candy. Sometimes I look off to the distant vale and discover a parade of three, five, or perhaps as many as ten brightly colored hot air balloons drifting like pollen on the breeze in my direction. In this already-magnificent Cotswold setting, it is a glorious, exciting sight!

Floating in from the north just as the sun is setting, the balloons often land in the vale to the south, too far away for me to see them touch down. But when the winds blow the balloons from south to north, they pass right over the village.

Because the village lies at the foot of the hill, there is always a frantic attempt by any low fliers to gain altitude so as to make it over the steep escarpment to the next valley and beyond. The quietness of distant balloons can be deceiving. When more hot air is needed for a quick ascent, thunderously loud blasts belch out of the balloon, like a fire-breathing monster on the loose.

It sounds and looks terribly frightening at such times, but the people inside the basket always seem to be of good cheer.

Sometimes they are so close that we exchange pleasantries. At other times they are sweeping by so rapidly that I find myself running up the village lane like a schoolboy just to keep up. Of course, my windedness as I rush up the steep hill at the far end of the village reminds me that I am not the energetic schoolboy I once was.

Yet the excitement spurs me on—past other villagers who have dashed out into their gardens to enjoy the sight; past the church with its squarish Norman steeple threatening to pierce the billowing nylon; and on to the top of the hill, where I catch my breath, take one last longing look, and then reluctantly bid farewell to these adventurers in their multicolored lighter-than-air ice-cream cones.

How I envy them! What it must be like up there, looking down on the patchwork quilt of green crops and bright-yellow summer rape fields, stitched together by threads of neatly trimmed hedgerows and seemingly endless dry-stone walls crisscrossing the countryside.

Sometimes I see them racing across the sky as if trying to catch the sunset. At other times I see them hovering motionless, like droplets of water on the underside of a spout which never seem to fall. Sometimes hurried, sometimes helpless, balloons are never alone up there—never totally free. They are always at the mercy of some invisible force.

That's why I have mixed feelings about going up in a balloon. You can never be totally in control. With my feet planted firmly on the ground, at least I *feel* like I'm in control. But up there, who knows? Up there I would be totally dependent upon the pilot, and he in turn is dependent upon winds and currents over which he has no control. And of course there are those church steeples to think about!

I suppose it's all about trusting the unseen—relying on forces we can't understand or control. Trusting other people is difficult enough, but trusting an invisible power is sometimes even more difficult.

When Thomas the doubter was finally convinced by the nailprints in Jesus' hands that Jesus had in fact risen bodily from the grave, Jesus told him, "Because you have seen me, you have believed; blessed are those who have not seen and yet have believed." Faith in the unseen is what faith is all about.

From my youth I have happily committed my trust to an unseen God. Even now, in most cases, I truly am a willing passenger. And so far the flight has been, if not always smooth, at least accompanied by an abiding sense of security. Over the years, I have been through storm and calm, through ups and downs; through the heartache of broken relationships, the passing of loved ones, the tears of defeat, the fear of loneliness, and the discouragement of my own fallibility. But somehow I keep flying. Somehow he lifts me higher. In the safety of his gracious providence he carries me over the rough times and shares with me the joys of a life lived by faith.

I confess that there are times when I find faith in God to be as confining as the basket hanging beneath the balloon. Sometimes I can't understand why I always have to be in *his* basket, or why I always have to do everything *his* way. Yet every time I truly turn my life over to God, I invariably forget the basket and find myself concentrating on the beauty. When I let God's invisible power take control, I am dependent, but oddly free. I am no longer in control, yet I am safe and secure in his leading.

The apostle Paul put it in terms of *freedom* versus *slavery*— the irony being that "slavery to God" provides greater freedom than what the world would think of as "freedom"! Writing to believers in the city of Rome, Paul said, "Now that you have been set free from sin and have become slaves to God, the benefit you reap leads to holiness, and the result is eternal life....Therefore, there is now no condemnation for those who are in Christ Jesus, because through Christ Jesus the law of the Spirit of life set me free from the law of sin and death."

Jesus himself talked about the kind of freedom that is *really* free. "If the Son sets you free, you will be *free indeed*," said Jesus. What makes us really free? In the words of Jesus "*the truth* will set you free." The truth that we are never in control even when we think we are. The truth that a life without God is the most fearful life anyone can live. The truth that the most fulfilled people in the world are those who have "let go and let God."

But "letting go" isn't always easy. So many things hold us back from flights of faith. For many of us, it's pride—perhaps the pride of having to admit that we've been wrong about God in the past. Possibly it's the fear of being disappointed if we really surrender ourselves to God's control. Or it's a relationship that might have to be sacrificed—or giving up the anger we harbor against God for something we've experienced that seems unjust. What is it that prevents *you* from climbing into the basket and taking off with God?

As I look around me, I sometimes think I see what balloonists must see all the time: other people looking on with envy, yet not quite sure they are ready to climb inside the basket. We all want the kind of faith that buoys up true believers, gives them assurance beyond themselves, and keeps them going even in the hard times. Usually, however, we are content to merely exchange pleasantries with God. If only *he* will get close enough to *us*, we think!

Sometimes we move beyond mere pleasantries. Sometimes the thought of actually being "up there" with God is sufficiently exciting to lead us on a wild chase in search of him through one religious avenue or another—as if somehow, through that distant chasing, we are truly involved in the experience.

But nothing can surpass the reality that settles in on us when we reach the point with God where we know beyond a shadow of doubt that he is in control. When we *really know* that we have nothing to fear! When we take that confident step and *actually get into the basket!* It is then, when we have let go of everything that holds us back, that we will know true freedom. And beauty. And breathtaking heights of exhilarating joy!

Chapter Three

"The tongue that
brings healing is
a tree of life, but a
deceitful tongue
crushes the spirit."

PROVERBS 15:4

Graffiti

I could hardly believe my eyes. But there it was—*graffiti!* Not in the center of London, or on the side of a commuter train, but here in this immaculately unspoiled countryside. Right in the heart of the Cotswolds!

Walking down from the Cotswold Way on a path leading to Stanton, I was still savoring the breathtaking view, eastward across the valley, of the picturesque village of Snowshill. One could be forgiven for thinking it was only a painting on a canvas, since no spot on earth could be that captivating. So imagine my surprise at seeing the unexpected contrast of spray-painted graffiti on an old piece of corrugated sheet metal. Nothing could have been more incongruous.

It wasn't just the graffiti. I've seen enough spray paint on school buildings, park benches, and highway overpasses to be immunized for a lifetime. But this was not your ordinary graffiti thoughtlessly scrawled on the side of a wall by contemptuous hooligans. This particular graffiti had a message as obscene as the visual desecration itself.

It was the worst kind of graffiti. It not only marred the beauty of the countryside, but also the character of the ones to whom it was directed. It was not just paint, but poison. Not simply desecration, but defamation.

I don't know how many persons from among the class of people being defamed actually saw the graffiti. Hopefully very few. But I think about the one or two who might have come down off the hill after a lovely day's walk, only to be confronted with the horror of this obscenity directed against them. It must have shattered their day, not to mention their esteem for fellow human beings!

Having just done some reading in the Psalms, I couldn't help but notice a parallel. In a particular collection of David's songs, I caught a glimpse of what anyone who is the target of hateful graffiti must feel. It was something that David apparently felt on many occasions. And, as I reflect on it, it is something I myself have felt: the hurt of hatred.

As king of Israel, it is not surprising that David would have his enemies—political enemies, military enemies, even personal enemies. Psalm after psalm tells us that David was hounded on every side:

> *Those who hate me without reason*
> *outnumber the hairs of my head;*
> *many are my enemies without cause,*
> *those who seek to destroy me.*

And for what was he hated? Sometimes simply for being a "man after God's own heart"!

> *For I endure scorn for your sake, and*
> *shame covers my face.*

In yet another psalm David prays to God for protection from his enemies, particularly those who speak evil of him:

*Hear me, O God, as I voice my
    complaint; protect my life from the threat
    of the enemy.
Hide me from the conspiracy of the
    wicked, from that noisy crowd of evildoers.
They sharpen their tongues like swords
    and aim their words like deadly arrows.
They shoot from ambush at the innocent
    man; they shoot at him suddenly,
    without fear.*

Notice that in both of these psalms David's enemies are not great armies coming against him with military strength. That kind of threat he could handle with ease. But in these psalms David's enemies are those who hurl venomous personal slander in his direction, whose weapons are their tongues. Like unexpected graffiti along a pristine walking path, their slander comes from out of nowhere, as in an ambush!

But who are David's enemies? In some instances they were people whom we too encounter—people who want to ridicule us because it makes them feel better about themselves and their own behavior. They are just waiting for us to slip and fall so that they can heap scorn on our struggling faith. If you've ever experienced such folks, then you can identify all too well with David's own agony:

*When I stumbled, they gathered in glee;
    attackers gathered against me when I
    was unaware.
They slandered me without ceasing.
Vindicate me in your righteousness, O LORD
    my God; do not let them gloat over me.
Do not let them think, "Aha, just what we
    wanted!" or say, "We have swallowed him
    up."*

But of course this is no more than we might expect from those who have no regard for anything spiritual. Should it be surprising that they would want to hurt us by gloating over any moral failings they might discover? How else can they justify their own sin but to point to ours?

Yet the verbal graffiti that hurts the most does not come from our enemies. Slander hurts most when it comes from those we love, and David knew that kind of scorn as well:

> If an enemy were insulting me, I could endure it;
> if a foe were raising himself against me, I could
>   hide from him.
> But it is you, a man like myself, my companion,
>   my close friend,
> with whom I once enjoyed sweet fellowship as
>   we walked with the throng at the house of
>   God.
>
> My companion attacks his friends; he violates his
>   covenant.
> His speech is smooth as butter, yet war is in his
>   heart;
> his words are more soothing than oil, yet they
>   are drawn swords.

One wonders whom David might have had in mind. Was it King Saul, who had befriended David, only to turn around and hurl a spear at him? Could it have been David's own son, Absalom, who conspired against his father? Whoever it might have been, David sees the beauty of his walk with God marred in the least likely place—in the eyes of a friend:

> Even my close friend, whom I trusted,
>   he who shared my bread,
>   has lifted up his heel against me.

Do you know that sickening feeling? Have you ever been betrayed by one of your closest friends? If he were an *enemy*, as David said, we could handle that. One can *expect* to find graffiti in certain places. It's when abuse and scorn come from those we love the most that we are thrown off guard and hurt the deepest. For all of us who have ever experienced that special pain, Julius Caesar summed it up best in his famous "Et tu, Brute?" Why should hatred and hurt ever come from our *friends!*

So what do we do when enemies slander us and friends betray us? Our natural reaction is usually the same as David's: to strike back, to seek revenge. David even tried to enlist God's help!

> *Pour out your wrath on them; let your*
> *fierce anger overtake them.*
>
> *Charge them with crime upon crime; do*
> *not let them share in your salvation.*
> *May they be blotted out of the book of*
> *life and not be listed with the*
> *righteous.*

The extent of David's pain—and ours—is reflected in David's uncharacteristic bitterness against the one who has slandered him:

> *May his days be few;*
> *May another take his place of leadership.*
> *May his children be fatherless and his wife a*
> *widow.*
> *May his children be wandering beggars; may*
> *they be driven from their ruined homes.*
> *May a creditor seize all he has;*
> *May strangers plunder the fruits of his labor.*

*May no one extend kindness to him or
take pity on his fatherless children.*

Have you ever been so hurt that you joined with David in
such sentiments? Have you responded angrily as a *victim* when
cutting remarks came your way? Lashing out at those who
would abuse us might vent our anger, but it is not likely to
heal any wounds, not even our own.

There is a more productive way to deal with offensive
verbal abuse. Graffiti itself gives us our first clue. In most
instances, graffiti can be covered over, never to be seen again.
Abusive words can also be covered. As Peter reminds us,
"Love each other deeply, because love covers over a multitude
of sins." So also says the proverb: "Hatred stirs up dissension,
but love covers over all wrongs."

Scorn, like graffiti, can often be covered over and forgotten.
But sometimes it can't. Words aren't so easily taken back. That
is when we must exercise godly forgiveness, letting compassion
help us to understand why the scorn came in our direction in
the first place. Maybe it was out of some deep-seated hurt in
the heart of the slanderer. Why else would a *friend*, in particular, turn on us?

It's reassuring to know that King David was not consumed
by vindictiveness, despite the harshness with which he
responded to character assassination. Out of the heart of this
same man came those memorable words of the 23rd Psalm:

*You prepare a table before me in the presence of
   my enemies.
You anoint my head with oil; my cup overflows.
Surely goodness and love will follow me all the
   days of my life,
and I will dwell in the house of the LORD forever.*

David might not have been able to deflect every cutting remark or silence every slander of his detractors. But no matter the adversity—even if in the presence of his enemies—David's security was in the Lord.

And what could be more strengthening to us than to realize that God knows *exactly* how we are hurt by other people's hatred? Even as Jesus hung in agony on the cross, he was still being slandered, scorned, and abused by his enemies. And *that* after having been betrayed by his *friends*! How did Jesus deal with this unprecedented verbal graffiti? In the same way that he calls us to respond: "Father, forgive them, for they do not know what they are doing."

"But it's easier said than done," you say. And I agree. But maybe we can draw from Jesus' example when in his hour of greatest trial he called out to God, "Father, into your hands I commit my spirit." I suspect it's not just coincidence that those words first appeared in one of David's psalms in which he faced the slander of his enemies and the contempt of his neighbors. For in those words—his last on the cross—we remember again that no one will ever bear greater slander or scorn than Jesus, and that our hope lies in turning it over to God.

If on your walk with God today you encounter some unexpected graffiti, don't let it catch you off guard. It's not *us* our enemies are targeting, but God himself, whose love has already covered it over for us. And as for the scorn which comes from our friends, it may hurt more, but who can we forgive if not our friends?

Besides, with friends it's usually only *thoughtless* graffiti that comes our way, and thoughtlessness is easy enough to cover. If we look real hard, we'll probably see that somewhere along the line someone has covered us with their love as well.

Chapter Four

"Among those who
approach me I will show
myself holy."

LEVITICUS 10:3

Church Bells

The church bells reverberated throughout the village with urgency. As I headed up the lane on my way into the hills just before sunset on a brightly lit summer's evening, I passed the church and the local bell-ringers. From the sound of the bells, the ringers were in rare form. More energy. More enthusiasm. More noise!

I love the sound of the bells, even when they are being rung only for practice, as today. Church bells are part of the rhythm of a small village. A village without church bells just isn't *English*! The ringing of the bells marks the most significant events in the life of the village: births, deaths, weddings, times of peace after periods of war. In our village the bells sometimes even ring for birthdays.

"Change-ringing," a style unique to England and dating back for at least three centuries, has a sound more like rhythmic peals than melodic tunes. It's a swirling sound. When the ringing is done with enthusiasm, the higher notes race down the scale to lower notes, and then again rapidly spill over the top, over and over again, creating an atmosphere of unrestrained excitement. It always makes you ask, What special occasion is happening? With six ringers pulling ropes to control the bells (some weighing three-quarters of a ton), listeners on the outside would hardly guess how much work is involved. All you hear is joy in the air, and an invitation to come join in!

As I went on up the lane, past the last cottages and across the fence into the Birts' sloping field, the sound of the bells followed along, as if a faithful companion. Higher and higher I climbed, until I could look down and see the church tower and the village far below. Oddly, the sound had hardly diminished. Each peal seemed to roll up the hill and explode in my ear. I wondered how far away people were able to hear the bells. Broadway? Snowshill? On other days I myself have been traversing the Cotswold Way and heard bells being rung in the village of Childswickham, three miles distant.

After my walk, I got to thinking about bells in relation to the church. I thought I recalled that there was little mention of bells in the Bible, but I double-checked just to make sure. As it turned out, I was surprised to find that bells are mentioned only twice. Yet even in those two brief Old Testament references, I discovered a rich message, itself worthy of some joyous bell-ringing!

The first passage which mentions bells is part of God's instructions for the building of the tabernacle and the making of its provisions for worship. Among the garments to be made for the priests—all described in great detail—are the sacred garments to be worn by Aaron the high priest. These included a breastpiece, an ephod, a robe, a tunic, a turban, and a sash. God said, "Make the robe of the ephod entirely of blue cloth....Make pomegranates of blue, purple and scarlet yarn around the hem of the robe, with gold bells between them. The gold bells and the pomegranates are to alternate around the hem of the robe. Aaron must wear it when he ministers."

You would think that, along with all those pomegranates, the bells might merely be decorative. But the attached explanation is more ominous than artistic: "The sound of the bells will be heard when he enters the Holy Place before the Lord and when he comes out, so that he will not die."

Could it really be? Tiny golden bells—a matter of *life and death*?

What we mustn't forget is that only the high priest entered the Holy Place, in the very presence of God. Were anyone else to do that, it would mean certain death. Mortal man dared not approach the God of all creation. Therefore even the high priest needed to "announce his coming" before the throne of the Almighty. And that may well be the symbolism of the bells—to "announce his coming" (not unlike the purpose of sleighbells and doorbells) and thereby bridge between the sacred and the secular, between the Holy One and the unholy one.

More than a thousand years pass before Scripture mentions bells again. This time it is found in Zechariah's prophecy, which looks forward to a day when the Savior of the world would revolutionize the nature of worship before God. And what a change it would be!

"On that day," says Zechariah, "'Holy to the Lord' will be inscribed on the bells of the horses, and the cooking pots in the LORD's house will be like the sacred bowls in front of the altar."

From bells on the high priest's robe to bells on horses! What could such a radical change possibly mean? Was there no longer to be a "holiness gap" between God and man? Could man now approach God without trepidation? Had the sacred and the secular become one? It's all a divine mystery—bells, sacred bowls, words saying, "Holy to the Lord." But the message for us is wonderfully clear.

Do you ever have the idea that you're not worthy of being loved by God? Have you ever felt so distanced from his love that it seems he doesn't care that you even exist? Have you ever thought that your sense of guilt is too great for God to do anything about?

The good news is that, with the coming of Jesus Christ into the world, we are no longer kept at arm's length from God. The role of the high priest—to bring our guilt and unworthiness before God—has been completed. Christ, who is your High Priest and mine, has offered himself as our sacrifice. Where we are unworthy, *he* is worthy on our behalf. Where we are unholy, *he* is the holy Lamb of God!

What it all means is that Jesus has given us unlimited access to God. There's no longer any need to feel like we can never reach out and touch God. Through the cross of Jesus, God has already reached out and touched *us*! At the very moment of Jesus' death, even "the curtain of the temple was torn in two from top to bottom." It once represented a curtain of separation, but no longer. Through our faith in Jesus Christ, we now approach with confidence the very throne of heaven!

Can you imagine what it would be like to pick up the phone and call the President of the United States on a direct line that goes right to his desk? How much more amazing, then, to know that we can enter directly into the heart of God! We have direct access. We've got his private number. When we call, he recognizes our voice. What a wonder it is to know that the God of Creation is calling us by name and saying, "How are you? How can I help you?"

When sin and guilt have separated us from God, we no longer need to "announce our coming," as if asking for permission to come into his presence. Jesus himself is our announcement! In one single hour of history, Jesus' crucifixion became the moment of greatest mourning, the moment of greatest celebration, and the moment of greatest peace to be witnessed by humankind. His death was the loudest anthem of bell-ringing the world has ever heard!

___

You must come to the Cotswolds, if for no other reason than to hear the bells. What a reminder they are that we can joyfully approach the Father and enter into his presence to find help in time of need—or simply to love him and praise him forever! Free access through Jesus restores the relationship that God himself longs for with each of us. Come celebrate that thought. Let the joybells within our hearts peal forth with unrestrained thanksgiving!

Chapter Five

"Is not wisdom
found among
the aged?
Does not long
life bring
understanding?"

JOB 12:12

The Old Church Wall

A s I begin my walk each day, I head up the village lane and past several quaint cottages, the old rectory, and the comfortably manicured grounds of the manor house. Not far along, on the right-hand side of the lane, is the gate and path leading up to the village church. The gate itself is part of an ancient stone wall—a very special stone wall which recently has taken on a new significance for me.

If you were to walk with me beside the wall for the first time, chances are it would catch your eye. You might even pause for a moment to appreciate how nicely it blends in with the churchyard above it, and how it adds dignity to the whole village scene. That was not always the case. A year or so ago, the wall was almost completely covered over by dirt, ivy, grass, and assorted weeds and brambles. Passersby had no idea what treasure lay beneath the camouflage.

That's when I determined to do my small bit of community service. Already there were other villagers doing their part, particularly the Keytes and the Clarkes, who faithfully look after the church grounds and village cemetery. The Buckland Manor crew and Dr. David Emory, physician-cum-farmer, mow the grassy verges on either side of the lane. Spritely Vick Sutton cleans up around the rectory grounds, and our tomato-grower, Chris Harvey, helps keep the playing field cut back. So it seemed high time that I make my own contribution, and I decided the old church wall might be just the thing.

With my gas-powered trimmer loudly whining away, I began a furious assault on the wall. It seemed like every crack and crevice had become a hiding place for clumps of unsightly intruders. The ivy clung tenaciously, and the pesky weeds played a stubborn game of hide-and-seek. But little by little, one by one, the beautiful stones were exposed to view. It wasn't until I stepped back after a couple of hours of hard labor that I saw the first large stretch of the wall fairly glimmering in the sunlight. It was like a finely polished gem!

Toward the end of the day I finally completed clearing the entire wall. Don and Mavis Keyte, who were working nearby in the cemetery, joined me for a brief respite. We looked on with pride at what now had become yet another lovely part of our beloved village. "Haven't seen the wall looking like that for years," Don beamed. It was a good feeling to have brought a thing of beauty from its once-disgraceful state to become the object of admiration.

For me the wall has become a constant reminder that within every person are gifts and talents—gemstones of character—just waiting to be uncovered. How many special people are there in my world whom I fail to appreciate because their inner qualities are not easily seen? I'm sure I'm not alone in focusing on the more superficial camouflage surrounding people, and in only rarely searching out what hidden human treasures might lie beneath the surface.

When I think of the old stone wall, I imagine the hundreds of stories it could tell about the generations which have come and gone since it was first built. If only stones could talk! But, of course, all around us are living stones who *can* talk. People who have seen it all, who have the ability to get back to basics, to true values. People whom I ignore on my busy road to success. But what a sense of timelessness they could lend to my own life, if only I would stop and listen!

Just the other day I met Bernard and his golden Labrador, Rob, on the path to the next village. Bernard (pronounced with the emphasis on the first syllable) grew up in that village and never traveled far from home. He's become hard of hearing now, and his walk has slowed considerably, but there's still a boyish twinkle in his eye. I love to hear him tell stories about what it was like in the Cotswolds during the war years.

More than that, I love to hear Bernard talk about the dogs in his life. You can tell even by the way he talks to Rob that Bernard's is a gentle, simple life. How I envy his uncluttered world with its warm memories and simple pleasures. As the passing years bring down the final curtain, life is reduced to little more than one man and his dog. What a treasure trove that is! Bernard's stories about "man's best friend" are really all about human relationships as well—stories of companionship, faithfulness, and unspoken trust.

There are other people, both old and young, who must have great difficulty sharing their inner beauty. And still others whose beauty has been hidden for years by circumstances over which they had little control—victims of child abuse, children of alcoholics, and so many individuals these days who are the painful products of families that failed to give them a proper sense of love and support.

That's what I find so remarkable about Jesus. He specialized in uncovering the beauty in people. It didn't matter to him whether he was talking to a beggar, or even a hated tax collector. Old or young, man or woman, rich or poor—to Jesus every person was important. Every person had his or her own story to tell. Every person had hurts that needed healing, and sins to be forgiven.

If a man was covered over with skepticism and doubt, Jesus brought out hidden faith. If a woman's inner beauty was hidden by shame and guilt, Jesus cut right through to a penitent heart yearning for release. *His* beauty became *their* beauty for all the world to see.

Once exposed to Jesus, no one was ever the same again. They were transformed in mind, body, and spirit. Oh, there would always be the occasional lapse in faith needing his reassurance, and there would always be that persistent sin in need of weeding out. But never again would a person touched by Jesus succumb completely to the insidious onslaught of this world.

The least likely people were often the very ones who were most grateful for Jesus taking the time to notice. There is no better example of such gratitude than the woman of whom it was tersely said that she had "lived a sinful life in that town." But this same "sinful woman" was the one who wiped Jesus' feet with her hair, kissed them, and poured perfume on them.

We don't know much about this woman. Perhaps she was indeed the prostitute that everyone seems to think she was. If so, what was it that led her to walk bravely into a dinner party being given for upper-crust socialites and dare to anoint Jesus in such a public way?

Had she earlier solicited Jesus as he passed her on the street corner? And had he surprised her by stopping momentarily to tell her of the Father's love, or by telling her (as he did the Samaritan woman at the well) a detail that no one but God could have known? Just imagine what she would have felt if he had said, "Your tears and prayer as you wept alone last night have gone up to God. You have a Father who loves you, and your sins are forgiven."

If Jesus had looked at her the way other men looked at her, he would have seen only an object for satisfying one's passions. But Jesus knew that her seductive clothing and brazen smile were only a pretense, masking the pain and hurt. Beneath the brambles and thorns of an empty life lay a woman of great value.

And, oh, how she blossomed at the first showering of forgiveness! It was not the stench of cheap perfume for which she is now remembered, but for the aroma of love which she poured out at the feet of the One who had cared enough to expose her inner beauty. She loved much because she was forgiven much! She was all the more precious in contrast to what she had been before Jesus took the time to notice her.

Uncovering the old stone wall by the church was well worth doing. But if we could only have the eyes of Jesus to see hidden beauty all around us. Then we too could experience the joy of partnership with Jesus, knowing that his love, working through us, can touch the hearts of people who are otherwise forgotten, people who need a sense of belonging and of usefulness, or just that bit of encouragement that will help them on their way.

Our lives are never the same when his love comes through us to others. The beauty we uncover in them may be the beginning of our own blossoming through the cultivation of Jesus' love within us. The words of George L. Johnson's insightful hymn capture it profoundly:

> Let the beauty of Jesus be seen in me,
> All his wonderful passion and purity;
> May His Spirit divine all my being refine;
> Let the beauty of Jesus be seen in me.

In the weeks and months since I first cleared off the church wall, I continue to look fondly on it every time I pass by. Here and there I see the ivy creeping back into familiar crevices, sneaking around as if I didn't notice. And the weeds are poking their heads up again, as if daring me to return with my mighty machine. But overall, the wall stands out proudly, providing a sense of graceful timelessness to all who pass by.

There's no question about it: Uncovering the old stone wall revealed a beauty I would never have known otherwise. But Jesus taught us how to reveal a far greater beauty in people—especially the most unlikely people. What a story they all have to tell! What hidden beauty they all have to share!

Chapter Six

"Where sin
increased, grace
increased all
the more."

Romans 5:20

Snowfall

The crunching of footsteps. Nature bedded down under a soft white blanket. A calming quiet. Snow has fallen in Buckland, and village life is transformed. Drifts covering the lane invite villagers to stay home today—to slow down, put a roaring fire in the fireplace, and enjoy the peacefulness. To look around and see the beauty. To feel the closeness.

Walking in the snow is hard going, but each step offers a reward. All around, the tall exposed branches on the trees are covered with a mixture of snow and ice, forming delicate lace patterns. Drifts of snow on stone walls swirl like icing on a wedding cake. Far from his burrow up in the hills, a rabbit hops through the fence behind one of the cottages. Tiny birds flutter about on a crest of frozen crystals, seeking out what food can be found. Their subtle coloring suddenly stands out brightly in stark contrast to the canvas of white beneath them.

What is it about snow that makes the world wake to its wonder? Perhaps its sheer novelty. Perhaps the magic of soft flurries coming down. Maybe it's all the fun we have in the snow—not just skiing, but snowmen, snowball fights, and snow ice cream! With so much to experience and enjoy, the falling of snow is a festival of fun.

For adults, the magic of snow is its ability to change us back into children—to once again experience wonder, to let ourselves play childlike games, to dream dreams, to build castles, to even allow ourselves to fall down with laughter! Snow is a time of innocence long lost. Each flake brings freshness, renewal, purging.

How many times have you wished you could start over again—to paint your life on a clean canvas, free of all the smudges that have hidden the beauty of the person you really are? I think that's what I like best about snow: It covers the ugliness and makes everything clean again. It softens the harshest terrain and brings beauty to the unsightly. It hides the footsteps of the past and invites us to walk where we've never walked before.

It shouldn't surprise us, then, that King David referred to snow when he wanted to make his life clean again. In the aftermath of his sin with Bathsheba, David pleaded for God's forgiveness, saying, "Wash me, and I will be whiter than snow." It was more than the embarrassment of having a public smudge on his life that David was trying to cover—more, even, than the acknowledgment of great sin before God. It was a haunting sense of guilt from which he could not escape. Hence David's prayer: "Have mercy on me, O God, according to your unfailing love; according to your great compassion blot out my transgressions. Wash away all my iniquity and cleanse me from my sin. For I know my transgressions, and my sin is always before me."

Do you know what it's like to have your sins *always before you*? To be *haunted by guilt*? Have you ever had the feeling that the sin you've committed is unforgivable? David had not only committed adultery, but he also had committed murder. How would it be possible to wash his hands of the blood he had shed? How could he feel clean again? How could he forget the sins of the past and get on with his life?

I dare say all of us have sins that haunt us—sins that are always before us, mirror-like, reminding us that we are not the persons we want to be. How then can we be free of guilt? How can we feel clean again?

Listen to what God has promised: "Though your sins are like scarlet, they shall be as white as snow; though they are red as crimson, they shall be like wool." Snow and wool—what an appropriate pairing! I saw them both on my walk today—and what I saw was God's grace.

Every day I cross a particular field that has an undulating, rolling terrain. Walking across it is like trying to walk on waves, one after another—up and down, up and down. But today in the snow the field looked flat, and with drifts filling in the troughs, even walking across it was easy.

What snow had done to a treacherous field reminds me of Isaiah's prophecy. As paraphrased in the Gospels, "Every valley shall be filled in, every mountain and hill made low. The crooked roads shall become straight, the rough ways smooth. And all mankind will see God's salvation."

Isn't that the nature of God's saving grace? His love fills in the spiritual depths of my weaknesses in order to pave the way forward. His life fills my emptiness and makes the rough times smooth.

I noticed something else on my walk today: Snow was all I could see. Whatever lay beneath the snow—whether mud-pools, thistles, or sheep droppings—was now hidden. None of us can undo the past; there are consequences from our sin that often linger far beyond the sin. But God's grace does what love does: Love covers!

No, grace is not a "cover-up," as in some criminal conspiracy that guilty men are anxious to hide. God's grace brings true forgiveness. And more than forgiveness, wonderful as that is, grace covers our hearts in their brokenness. Grace is gentle and caring. It covers like a healing bandage to protect us from further harm. Most of all, his grace gives us hope that we can walk where we've never walked before—*above* the mud, *above* the muck, where a life lived in Christ is "white as snow."

But just as I was exhilarating in the snow around me, I heard the distressed sounds of sheep, desperate to find grass, which, like everything else, had been covered by the snow. Then I saw the sheep running for the hay that had been put out in a feeder box across the way. Suddenly I saw the other side of grace: Grace not only covers, but it also provides.

Fortunately, God doesn't just paint pretty pictures with snow and then leave me to starve. As the Good Shepherd, the Lord of Grace feeds the hunger in my soul and keeps me going. With David, I too can say, "The Lord is my shepherd, I shall not be in want," for by God's grace I am both covered and nourished, forgiven and sustained, innocent and secure. How great is God's faithfulness! His mercies are new every morning!

Tonight the snow is still falling, and I can hardly wait until morning. Like an excited child, I will rush to the window—as if for the very first time—to catch sight of the snow once again. But it won't be just the snow I see; it will be the grace of God in me.

Chapter Seven

"Do not imitate
what is evil but
what is good."

3 JOHN 11

IMITATING

Jacob Sheep

They're so different. Odd, really—all creamy-colored with chocolate spots. Certainly not your typical sheep! In fact, I can't remember seeing them on the hillside before this year. Known as "Jacob sheep," these speckled fellows have somehow made their way to the Cotswolds. Speckled is interesting, but I think I prefer a more uniform color. Sheep are supposed to be woolly white, aren't they? Or at least woolly black! *Speckled* is another matter altogether.

Maybe if the Jacob sheep were in a field all by themselves they might look better. But mixed in with the others, the Jacob sheep spoil the picture. Somehow it's not England anymore. Perhaps the Hebrides, or the Mediterranean, which are home to this unusual breed. But not *England!*

Sometimes I wonder how many people know the origin of the name "Jacob sheep." Some folks might be surprised to learn that it comes from the Bible. Since I was a child I've known the story of Jacob and his speckled sheep, but I must admit that the story has become even more intriguing now that I have seen these interesting creatures.

You'll recall that Jacob fell in love with Rachel, but was tricked by her father into first marrying the older sister, Leah, who was still unmarried. When Jacob finally was allowed to marry Rachel, his father-in-law, Laban, continued to prove himself a scoundrel. After 14 years of taking Laban's abuse and dishonesty, Jacob decided to leave Laban's employ. In the end, Jacob proposed a settlement that was remarkably fair, considering the number of years Jacob had worked for Laban.

The idea was simple enough. At that time in Syria, with few exceptions the sheep were white. Jacob asked as his share of the flocks only the sheep that were speckled and spotted. Laban agreed, but immediately tried to cheat Jacob by having his sons cull out all the streaked and spotted sheep and take them away so that none would be left for Jacob.

Encouraged by a dream from God, Jacob devised an intricate plan of breeding through which more and more speckled sheep would be produced. He was directed to make sure that the mating of the sheep and goats was done in the presence of multicolored objects.

In some instances he cut dark wood branches so as to show white streaks, and then placed them near the watering troughs where the sheep mated. Sometimes mating was permitted only in the presence of other speckled sheep. The result either way was that Jacob's speckled flocks rapidly multiplied, making him a prosperous man.

As I walk among the Jacob sheep on the hill above the village, I cannot help but wonder about Jacob's method of breeding. Did what the sheep look at as they were mating really affect the color of the offspring?

What intrigues me even more is that *human nature* does indeed mimic Jacob's method of breeding. What we act out in our lives is very often dictated by what we choose to focus our attention on.

Think, for example, of Jesus' statement about looking, lusting, and sinning: "I tell you that anyone who looks at a woman lustfully has already committed adultery with her in his heart." Our eyes feed our imagination, and what we imagine can be as spiritually lethal as what we might actually do.

Little wonder that Jesus made a direct connection between the eye and the consequences of what it allows us to sinfully imagine. "If your right eye causes you to sin," Jesus went on to warn, "gouge it out and throw it away. It is better for you to lose one part of your body than for your whole body to be thrown into hell."

Sometimes we say that the eyes are the windows to the soul. Jesus put it only slightly differently: "The eye is the lamp of the body. If your eyes are good, your whole body will be full of light. But if your eyes are bad, your whole body will be full of darkness. If then the light within you is darkness, how great is that darkness!" Clearly, Jesus is not talking here about impaired vision. Once again he is making a tie between what we see and how it affects what is in our heart.

Windows without screens can let in a lot of nasty creatures! There is a sense in which our eyes likewise are screens guarding our inner being. Without their filter, our hearts can become dangerously polluted. Perhaps that is what the writer of the proverb had in mind when he wrote, "Above all else, guard your heart, for it is the wellspring of life."

The point is that what we allow ourselves to see has a profound impact on what we think and what we do. If Jacob's unusual method of breeding is somewhat suspect, there is nothing suspect at all about the progression from seeing to imagining to imitating. The only question can be, What sinful activity are we *imitating* in our lives simply because we have allowed ourselves to *see* it?

The psalmist encourages us to be like the ordinary sheep which Jacob placed in pens to mate in the presence of speckled sheep. "Look to the Lord and his strength; seek his face always," he urges. As we look to the Lord and seek his face, we are transformed. His character becomes our character; his higher ways our ways; his divine nature our own Spirit-filled godliness.

The apostle John projects this process of transformation even into the future, to the time of the Lord's second coming. "Dear friends," John exhorts, "now we are children of God, and what we will be has not yet been made known. But we know that when he appears, we shall be like him, for we shall see him as he is." Since we will be like him at his coming, we can begin to become like him now. As John reminds us, "Everyone who has this hope in him purifies himself, just as he is pure."

Is there a more lofty passage in all of Scripture than the apostle Paul's call to purity? "Whatever is true, whatever is noble, whatever is right, whatever is pure, whatever is lovely, whatever is admirable—if anything is excellent or praise-worthy—think about such things."

How does that call to purity compare with our day-to-day thinking? Do we look on what is noble, pure, and lovely, or are we, like so many around us, fixing our gaze on what is base, filthy, and ugly? Have we stopped lately to consider that what we regularly watch on prime-time television and read in popular novels is nothing less than what, only one generation ago, would have been considered pornography? Are we watching "speckled morality" while harboring the hope that somehow we will reproduce woolly-white purity?

James asks us a hard question: "Can both fresh water and salt water flow from the same spring? My brothers, can a fig tree bear olives, or a grapevine bear figs? Neither can a salt spring produce fresh water." James insists that we can't have it both ways. To *be* pure, we must first *look upon* what is pure. If what we allow ourselves to see is impure, then at best we will produce mixed results.

It's reassuring to know that we have a significant advantage over the sheep in Jacob's pasture: God never sets temptation in front of us. Certainly there are speckled images on every hand—in movies, in books, and in the unrighteous living of the crowd around us—but these images are not from God.

Our greatest gift from God was Jesus "the Lamb." The pure Lamb. The righteous Lamb in whom was no sin. The Lamb on whom we can fix our eyes and whom we can imitate freely with the confident assurance of being transformed into the likeness of his glory!

Chapter Eight

"Each with his
sword at his side,
prepared for the
terrors of the night."

SONG OF SONGS 3:8

Warplanes

There is a particular spot in the hills high above the valley floor from which I can survey the entire breadth of the Vale of Evesham. Especially on clear days, that lofty perch provides an awe-inspiring bird's-eye view of life below. The village of Stanton, off to the south, and the village of Laverton, at the foot of the hills, are miniature in scale. Cars traveling on the Winchcombe road look like they could have come straight out of a child's toybox.

From that height there's an almost Godlike perspective. It's a great place to ponder, reflect, and meditate. Up there in quiet reverie, I can sort out the big issues of life. Most of all, there is a wonderful sense of quiet and solitude.

But just at the moment I am completely mesmerized by the tranquility of my lofty perch, the serenity of my contemplation is violently shattered by a screeching, thunderous roar that almost literally has me diving for cover. My whole body reacts instinctively, as if to a threatened attack. And the image of *attack* is precisely the right image. What I have just experienced is the startling apocalypse of warplanes practicing low-level contour flying, often so close that I can actually see the pilots' helmets!

On some days the parade of terror seems endless. One after another, the skies unleash a menacing menagerie of Tornadoes, Jaguars, Warthogs, and Harriers, sometimes joined by swift-flying F-111's and F-14's. From my vantage point high on the hillside, it seems strange to look *down* on planes engaged in mock dog fights and bombing runs.

Apparently the Royal Air Force has chosen the Cotswolds as a prime practice area, perfectly suited because of its rapidly changing terrain. And I guess that being able to swoop off the top of the hills down into the valley below must provide a real thrill for the crews—like exuberant children swishing again and again down a long, slippery slide. I keep wondering if they know what shivering chills they send down my spine as they roar over my head, or ever see the look of alarm on the faces of the sheep grazing nearby.

As you think about it, isn't that how life often plays itself out? One minute everything is calm, peaceful, and secure; the next minute we're under some kind of an attack from out of the blue. Maybe it's those chilling words, "I'm afraid you've got cancer." Or a wife's worst nightmare—the hurriedly scribbled note saying, "I'm leaving you for someone else." Maybe it's the boss with a pink slip in his hand, or the juvenile officer standing at the front door with your son in tow. Or the teenager who announces she's pregnant, or the midnight call informing you that your father or mother has just had a stroke.

The day had been perfect, hadn't it? Then came the bad news, like an F-14 swooshing down from the sky to shake your body and nerves to the very bone! Whatever the bad news, it fairly took your breath away. It was too late for anticipation; you couldn't run away from it; there was no escaping the terror.

I suspect this is exactly how Job must have felt when his whole world suddenly crumbled around him. Flocks and herds, servants, even his sons and daughters—all suddenly dead. What had he done to deserve such a catastrophe? Nothing, really. As with Job, so with us all: Death happens—and disease, and alienation, and fear, and loneliness. At one time or another they all come screeching into our lives. Trouble never phones ahead for an appointment.

We've spoken here of the catastrophic, but if you're like me, some of the worst sneak attacks are far more subtle. For example, there are those bouts of loneliness that surprise us— sometimes in the midst of a crowd on a happy occasion. How could we possibly be lonely with so many friends around? Or just one of those nonproductive days when everything else points to success. Why is there no energy, no creativity, no enthusiasm? It seems such a waste of time and opportunity! Add your own surprise attacks to the list. Might they include unexpected depression? A sudden outburst of temper? Previously unknown feelings of jealousy?

Nothing is more terrifying than those *spiritual* intruders— those secret thoughts, forbidden relationships, and fleshly desires that drag us down. Those moments of weakness that attack us just at the point when we think we are strong. Even those times when we get so tired of fighting off temptation that we are tempted to let the intruders win, hoping in vain that we can find peace in compromise.

To some degree, of course, we *can* have peace through compromise. But it's not a true or lasting or fulfilling peace. Why? Because life is all about conflict. Peace comes not in the *cessation* of conflict but in learning how to *deal* with conflict. The peace process begins on the familiar battleground of our own hearts.

Behind every war, battle, or bitter personal conflict lies a spiritual dimension. James said it best in his epistle: "What causes fights and quarrels among you? Don't they come from your desires that battle within you?"

It's those sneak-attack desires that bring conflict: greed, covetousness, pride—the whole long list. And it is only there—in being *prepared* to fight the battles against destructive personal desires and the fear of unexpected calamities—that the road to true peace will be found. The peace of God comes to us when we use the quiet times in our life to turn our hearts over to God so that he can prepare us for whatever struggles we face.

I realize that the notion of "quiet times" means different things to different people. For some it is a set time of daily devotionals, including Bible reading and prayer. For others it's a time of solitude and reflection on one's life in light of what we know to be God's will. Perhaps it's reading a book like this one, letting someone else suggest thoughts to ponder.

However we approach them, our quiet times will take on increased meaning when we begin to see that, out of those special times with him, we will emerge better prepared for the spiritual battles which lie ahead.

Our "quiet time" may be a particularly wonderful day with the family—so that when loneliness strikes us we have something to look back on to remind us that we are surrounded by those who love us. Our "quiet time" may be yesterday's mountaintop experience, so that when today's discouragement swoops in we are not in as low a valley as we might otherwise be. Our "quiet time" may be a friend's gentle response to something we've done foolishly—so that, when our own temper threatens to explode, we can be stronger in controlling it. Are we alert to all the "quiet times" God brings our way each day? He is helping us to be prepared. He doesn't want any of us to be caught off guard.

Never are we better armed and ready than when we remind ourselves of how Jesus responded to sneak attacks. When

Satan repeatedly threatened, Jesus quickly turned to familiar Scripture: "It is written," he said over and over. That is why reading our Bibles is so important. It tells us how godly people before us have dealt with our same struggles, and how God is always on our side.

And then there is that other avenue of assurance we are given. In the face of danger, Jesus went to the Father in prayer. Indeed, how often he went off to pray "in a quiet place" just before some special challenge.

Spiritual quiet times are the first line of defense against life's sneak attacks. They are times for rearming ourselves, for shoring up our defenses, for calling in prayer support. They are times for putting on "the full armor of God"—truth, righteousness, and faith. Our defensive armor is the assurance of our salvation. Our weapon of counterattack is the "sword of the Spirit, which is the word of God."

My walks in the Cotswolds are a never-ending search for moments of peace and tranquility. But when screeching warplanes disturb my quiet reverie, I begin to appreciate ever more fully that true peace comes only from God. The real war is not without, but within. I don't know what "spiritual warplanes" dive-bomb into your own life, but everyone knows that same inner struggle for peace within and that longing for harmony with those around us.

Would that we could make daily low-level sorties over the spiritual terrain of a life lived in Christ. Perhaps then we could know what it means to have true "peace on earth"—to know that, whatever intruder comes along to disturb our life, it can't win. To know that the greatest battle of all time has already been fought and won, and that through faith in him who has triumphed over death itself, the same victory is ours!

Chapter Nine

"Lest the cross
of Christ be
emptied of
its power."

1 CORINTHIANS 1:17

Jumbo the Elephant

One of the great joys of living in the English country-side is being able to share it with my friends. Visitors from Los Angeles, Nashville, Houston, and New Orleans are absolutely thrilled at the sight of the Cotswolds. They love the villages, the tea shops, the antiques—and most of all, the serenity. Get them away from crowded freeways, urban sprawl, and hectic schedules, and they become trans-formed, renewed people.

That's why I like to take my visitors up into the hills for a walk. There's even an ample supply of walking sticks and "Wellies" in various sizes to accommodate every need. And usually our walks together turn out to be one of the highlights of their trip. Rambling through the hills slows them down, allows them to breathe, and lets them catch a glimpse of the solitude which I enjoy day in and day out.

Two-thirds of the way up the hill which leads from the back of the manor house is a large, bulging, grass-covered mound surrounded by an almost-elaborate iron-bar fence. The mound is probably 15 by 25 feet across, and some four to five feet high where the hill drops away beneath it. It's so unusual that my friends invariably want to know what it is.

As I heard it, back in the thirties a circus was visiting in the town of Evesham, six miles away to the west. During the week that the circus was playing, a fire broke out in the town hall, and Jumbo the elephant was called into action to lift a beam which had fallen and trapped the local mayor. The mayor was saved, but the stress apparently was too much for Jumbo, and he died. In appreciation for Jumbo's heroism, the town council decided to give Jumbo a proper burial. With great effort he was brought to Buckland, hauled up the hill, and given this wonderful gravesite overlooking the town of Evesham in the distance.

Or at least that is the highly improbable story I love to tell, and it's the highly improbable story my friends love to hear! Whether it's the sound of the water running under the grassy mound, or merely my smug satisfaction which eventually betrays me, it's not long before eager belief turns into skeptical doubt. It is then that I have to confess that I've been leading them on, and that the grassy mound is nothing more than a water reservoir.

The amazing thing is how the story always works! Despite its great improbability, there is just enough possibility to it that people are willing to believe it—if only for a moment. Somehow I think that they *want* to believe it. After all, what a great story it would be if it were true! And it also helps that it involves a circus. How we all love a circus!

I think I see something of Jumbo in the Gospel accounts. During his ministry, Jesus had thrilled the crowds with the miracles he had performed. Whether turning water to wine, healing the sick, raising the dead, or walking on water, nothing was too difficult for Jesus. And the people wanted to make him King; they wanted to believe the wonder worker. How we all love a circus. How we all love a show!

When it comes to wanting the miraculous, nothing has changed. Still today, it's the magic of Christmas and the excitement of Easter that pulls in the crowds. Those who call themselves believers may never darken the doorway of the church at any other time, but they'll be scrambling for seats at the Christmas pageant or Easter sunrise service.

In that light, the story of Jumbo has caused me to appreciate like never before one of the most curious statements in all of Christian literature. It is found in the apostle Paul's first letter to the Christians in Corinth, where Paul makes a particular point of emphasizing that "we preach Christ crucified." Christ *crucified*? What a strange statement in connection with the life of Jesus. Why not Christ *born*, or Christ *resurrected*, or even Christ *ascended*? With all the wonderful things we could proclaim about Jesus, why would we ever focus in on something so seemingly negative?

Initially, not even Jesus' own disciples could understand the cross. They had envisioned Jesus reigning as a political king, with they themselves holding the most important positions in his kingdom. Like so many of us, they too were looking for the spectacular. Their disillusionment at the foot of the cross was not unlike the disillusionment of people today who are attracted by the razzle-dazzle brand of Christianity offered on every hand, but who quickly discover that this razzle-dazzle offers little of substance when the hard times come along.

With the miracle worker left hanging on the cross, all that is left—from a human perspective—is emptiness and foolishness. The magic is gone. There's no circus, no show.

And that is where you and I come in. There are times when, like Jesus, we too find ourselves bearing a cross! Times when we too know what it is like being betrayed by our friends and rejected by those who ought to love us the most. Times when we too know suffering—whether the agonizing pain of arthritis or perhaps the pain of separation from a loved one.

Hardly ever are we very far from moments when we feel powerless, helpless, and vulnerable to events around us that we simply can't control.

It's at those very times, when we find ourselves feeling fearful, alone, and helpless, that we need to hear the reassuring words of Paul: "The foolishness of God is wiser than man's wisdom, and the weakness of God is stronger than man's strength." What an incredible thought! Because of his own crucifixion, Jesus knows *exactly* how we feel! And it is in just such moments that he lifts us up—he on his cross, we on ours.

The cross of Jesus does something else for us that takes on increased importance when all around us we hear a problem-free gospel being preached. The cross properly sorts out idealism and realism in our Christian walk. The cross points out the difference between how we *want to believe* the Christian life will be and how it is *in truth*. We want wholeness, but we find that very wholeness in our brokenness. We want strength, but we discover that our strength comes only through our weakness.

Among the many ironies of a trusting faith, we learn through our daily walk with God that the meek really do inherit the earth, and that the kingdom of heaven really does belong to the poor in spirit. In the topsy-turvy kingdom of Christ we find all our values turned on their head: "The first shall be last, and the last shall be first"; "He who is least among you is the greatest"; "Whoever loses his life for my sake will find it."

The Christian walk is not always the world's success story. God doesn't always give us the Cadillac or dream house we want, nor the baby we've tearfully prayed for, nor the life of a loved one we desperately want to snatch from the grip of death. Not all marriages are the happily-ever-after unions of romantic fairy tales. No, even for Christians, life is not always ideal. We have no immunity from death and taxes, and, contrary to rumor, God *doesn't* always provide a miracle.

It's from the cross that we learn what a Jumbo-sized mistake it is to always expect a miracle. We don't preach a *rescued* Christ but a *crucified* Christ. Jesus did not miraculously *escape* the cross; he *endured* it! He conquered it through faith, and that's how it can be for us. If we can't *escape* the pain we are experiencing, at least we have the assurance that we can *endure* it. If we can't *understand* our suffering, at least we know we can *overcome* it.

It should be wonder enough that the miracle is not in changed *circumstances* but in our changed *attitude* about whatever circumstances we find ourselves in. The miracle of Calvary was not in Jesus coming down off the cross, as his tormentors challenged him to do. The miracle was how God turned what should have been the defeat of the cross into victory; crucifixion into glorification!

We too can share in the true miracle of the cross: learning to surrender so that we might be exalted! Learning to humble ourselves under the mighty hand of God so that he might lift us up! Hymnwriter J. R. Wreford expressed it sublimely in this timeless verse:

> *When my love for man grows weak,*
> *When for stronger faith I seek,*
> *Hill of Calvary! I go*
> *To Thy scenes of fear and woe.*
>
> *There behold His agony,*
> *Suffered on the bitter tree;*
> *See His anguish, see His faith,*
> *Love triumphant still in death.*
>
> *Then to life I turn again,*
> *Learning all the worth of pain;*
> *Learning all the might that lies*
> *In a full self-sacrifice.*

Unlike Jumbo the elephant, Jesus is not just some good story that somebody made up. And it's Christ *crucified* that we have to thank for the difference. The true miracle of the cross is not some shallow sense of the spectacular which gives us warm fuzzies once or twice a year, but the undeniable fact of Jesus' presence in our lives when the going gets tough.

Whatever our cross may be, his weakness becomes our strength, and his triumph becomes our hope!

Chapter Ten

"As long as the earth
endures, seedtime and
harvest, cold and heat,
summer and winter,
day and night will
never cease."

GENESIS 8:22

Seasons

It's the first day of June, and summer is in full stride. My walk today to Stanton was an impressionistic portrait painted from a palate of multicolored hues and soft textures. The backdrop was green—deep green, light green, even bright green—all in contrast to the clear blue sky which crisply bordered the splash of green on the horizon. In the foreground were chestnut trees sporting their smart red lanterns and plush-carpeted fields accented with tiny buttercups; everywhere along the way were pink-and-white-blossomed hawthorn, delightfully delicate red campions, and creamy flowers of the wild cow parsley.

Summer reaches out to touch you. Not like winter, which stands off coldly. Nor even spring, which is exciting yet merely flirtatious. As you walk along in summer, you are fairly embraced by the foliage. The tall slender grasses in the meadows reach up to your waist. In the narrow paths, nature's flowery fingers trace your passing figure. In sheltered lanes, beneath overhanging limbs now laden with leaves and summer vines, you are surrounded as if in a tunnel of love—nature's love.

How I love summer in England! And spring. And autumn. And, yes, even winter! Each season has its own magic, its own gift. And with each season comes something special. I pity those who never experience the change of seasons. How do they ever mark the progress of their lives? What do they have to look forward to? What lessons can they learn about the ever-unfolding mystery of nature and its message about the seasons of human existence?

Through the cycle of the seasons we discover that life has meaning, and balance, and the challenge of change. It's not just spring, summer, autumn, and winter. The seasons of life begin joyously with the *spring* of birth, seek ascendancy in the *summer* of youth, enjoy repose in the gentle *autumn* of retirement, and find completion—no, expectancy!—in death's *winter*. That's what life is all about. So too the ongoing spring of humankind's regeneration throughout the centuries—and especially at the resurrection of the faithful, the Eternal Season where there will be no winter of death, but only the eternal life of spring, summer, and autumn all wrapped up in one glorious season forever!

Seasons tell us much about God, including the very fact that God exists. It was the apostle Paul who reminded us that God "has not left himself without testimony: He has shown kindness by giving you rain from heaven and crops in their seasons."

Left to itself, how would nature have come up with the idea of seasons? Or managed to organize every part of the universe to make it happen? Or maintained such a precise schedule throughout recorded history? God exists all right! It was he who said, "Let there be lights in the expanse of the sky to separate the day from the night, and let them serve as signs to mark seasons and days and years."

The psalmist had no doubt that seasons were a gift from God. "It was you," he acknowledged, "who set all the boundaries of the earth; you made both summer and winter." All of nature revels in the gift of the seasons! "Even the stork in the sky knows her appointed seasons, and the dove, the swift and the thrush observe the time of their migration."

Seasons in nature are merely reminders of the rhythm and cycle of the seasons in our own lives. Wise Solomon captured it best:

> There is a time for everything,
> and a season for every activity under heaven.

Naturally, we are more familiar with seasons like spring and summer, but each *day* also has its own seasons which correspond to the rhythms of our fluctuating needs and desires. Each day has its own time of awakening, busy activity, nourishment, excitement, and rest.

Each day, each week, each season, each lifetime has purpose and meaning. So too each feeling and experience within those time frames. It was through that well-known series of contrasts that Solomon reminds us of the context into which we can place *all* of our feelings and experiences. Everything fits—whether a time to be born or a time to die, whether a time to love or even a time to hate.

So too the other contrasts. If there is a time to plant, there is also a time to uproot. If there is a time to kill, there is also a time to heal. Whether planting or uprooting, killing or healing, given the proper context, they each have their place.

Is there any reason to believe that the contrasting seasons in our own lives should be any different? If we want times of laughter, can we really think there will be no times of weeping? If there is a time to embrace, should we be surprised to learn that there are times when we ought to refrain from embracing? And if there is a time to keep, is there not also a time to let go of things that hold us back? Put differently, how do we know what to *let go of* until we know what to *keep*? Finding balance in life comes from appreciating the contrasts.

Have you ever noticed that opposite seasons help to define their counterparts? What we know of winter is partly in contrast to what we know of summer. Seasons may be quite different, but rarely are they totally unrelated. Joy and sadness, for example, are not the same, but joy is best known in contrast to sadness. Think too how life takes on added meaning in the face of death, and how silence seems golden when there's been too much speech.

The thing about seasons is that they always come and go. Here today, gone tomorrow, and back again in their own time. If we're talking about good times, naturally we could wish that the season of happiness would never end. Of course, that is never the case; happiness invariably comes to an end. But look what hope this perspective gives us for the opposite season of sadness: If sadness comes our way, we can know in advance that it too will go away. Here today, gone tomorrow!

So it goes for bereavement, separation, rejection, shame, discouragement, suffering, hatred, persecution, and the whole long list of things we would rather never face. In Psalm 30 David captures hope in a bottle: "Weeping may remain for a night, but rejoicing comes in the morning!" Who more than David would know about tragedy being transformed into triumph?

The writer of Lamentations, probably Jeremiah, expressed it beautifully. In the changing seasons of life, says the writer, the steadfast love of the Lord never ceases. His mercies never come to an end; they are new every morning. Great is his faithfulness!

These words are all the more surprising because they were written in the wake of Jerusalem's fall. How could Jeremiah have any hope after seeing men, women, and children brutally cut down in the city streets by the marauding Babylonian hordes?

Undoubtedly it was because Jeremiah knew that, whether in good times or bad, God had always been faithful. If there had been a time of war, Jeremiah knew there would also be a time of peace. God had been faithful from the very beginning of the nation of Israel, when it was yet in Abraham's loins. Without God's faithfulness, Israel would never have been.

Every Jew knew the story by heart: "By faith Abraham, even though he was past age—and Sarah herself was barren— was enabled to become a father because he considered him faithful who had made the promise." It didn't matter that Abraham and Sarah were far beyond the season of having children. God had promised, God was faithful, and God delivered!

Is yours a season of barrenness? Does it seem like your life is at a standstill and unproductive? God promises *fruitfulness*, and he is faithful who promised!

What Jew could forget the great exodus from Egypt, where the Israelites had been enslaved in bondage? God had not forgotten them. "The Israelites groaned in their slavery and cried out, and their cry for help because of their slavery went up to God. God heard their groaning and he remembered his covenant with Abraham, with Isaac and with Jacob." When all seemed lost, God remained faithful to Israel.

Is yours a season of bondage? Is there something so overpowering in your life that you feel helplessly enslaved? God promises *freedom*, and he is faithful who promised!

The time of the wilderness wandering must have given Israel some second thoughts about God's faithfulness. Where was the promised land that God had talked about? Yet it was not God's unfaithfulness but Israel's own sin that kept them wandering in the desert. The amazing thing is that God ultimately was faithful in providing the land despite Israel's defiant rebellion. Just how faithful is God? Paul says that even "if we are faithless, he will remain faithful, for he cannot disown himself."

Is yours a season of sin and wandering away from God? Do you find yourself in some vast spiritual wasteland, repeating the same sins over and over again? God promises *forgiveness*, and he is faithful who promised!

There would be other times when Israel would be cast from God's presence, only to be brought back from captivity and bondage. Even before Jerusalem was brought to her knees by the Babylonians, and God's people taken away into a foreign land, God promised that he would be faithful in restoration. "The ransomed of the Lord will return," said God through Isaiah. "They will enter Zion with singing; everlasting joy will crown their heads. Gladness and joy will overtake them, and sorrow and sighing will flee away." Israel would not always be exiled in a foreign land, nor weep by the rivers of Babylon. Deliverance was at hand!

Is yours a season of exile and alienation? Is *their* question *your* question: "How can we sing the songs of the Lord while in a foreign land?" If so, God promises *restoration*, and he is faithful who promised!

Whatever struggles you might be experiencing, God's promises endure in the changing seasons of life. Whether in good times or bad, God is always with us. "Know therefore that the Lord your God is God; he is the faithful God, keeping his covenant of love to a thousand generations of those who love him and keep his commands!"

Seasons come and seasons go. So do the passages of our lives. But Jesus Christ, the Faithful One, is the same yesterday and today and forever. With God there are no seasons. And because of that, there need be no season without God.

Swift to its close ebbs out life's little day;
Earth's joys grow dim, its glories pass away;
Change and decay in all around I see;
O Thou who changest not, abide with me!

I need Thy presence every passing hour;
What but Thy grace can foil the tempter's power?
Who, like Thyself, my guide and stay can be?
Through clouds and sunshine, O abide
with me!

—Henry F. Lyte

Chapter Eleven

"Death and Destruction
are never satisfied,
and neither are the
eyes of man."

PROVERBS 27:20

Dream House

For several years now I've been enchanted by a particular house in the village of Stanton. Perhaps I should say that I'm enchanted by the *setting* of the house, because I've never even been inside the house itself. But its overall ambience is glorious—my perfect "dream house"!

The gardens alongside the road lead to the back of the property, where there is a lovely little lake graced with swimming ducks, a commanding willow tree at the water's edge, and just the right beached boat to complete the postcard picture. Overlooking the lake and garden is an ornate Victorian glass conservatory. The house itself is a large two-story Cotswold stone structure, with slate roof and mullioned windows. Dignified. Traditional. Stately.

I had always told myself that this is the kind of house no one would ever sell. Surely it would be handed down in the family as an heirloom from one generation to the next. So imagine my excitement when I first saw the "For Sale" sign!

But my excitement was short-lived, because I soon realized just how much of a *dream* house it really was. The asking price was clearly outside my pocketbook—not to mention my bank account or even some loan officer's wildest generosity. It might as well have been Windsor Castle that I wanted to buy! But still today, I pause at the gate, look wistfully, and only reluctantly head for home.

"Reluctantly head for home?" Did I really say *reluctantly* with reference to my little cottage in Buckland that I have come to love? The cottage that, only a few short years ago, was *then* the house of my dreams? Even today I can't drive down the lane and see my little place without bursting with pride: "That's *my* cottage! Can you believe it? I actually live in that cute little place!"

How silly I am to drool over my "dream house" in Stanton when I already live in a "dream house" in Buckland. And if the house in Stanton is "the perfect house"—all that I would *ever* want—then why do I still occasionally stop at the estate agent's window looking at yet other houses for sale? Do I never tire of wanting more? Will I never be content with what I have?

Usually I am able to count my blessings and find great contentment in the abundance with which I have been blessed. I know that in the eyes of a world mostly wallowing in poverty, I am rich. So how could I ever ask for more?

Being "rich," whatever one's level of affluence, is no guarantee of contentment. To the contrary, it simply whets the appetite for having more. I remember impoverished student days when I hardly knew the meaning of greed—just survival! Having *more* than we need has a way of raising our expectations of *what* we need.

The wise (and exceedingly rich) King Solomon told it like it is: "Whoever loves money never has money enough; whoever loves wealth is never satisfied with his income."

Those who constantly want more surely must have some twinge of conscience for all their material lust and avarice. This is the person Jesus described as the man who tore down his barns to build bigger ones. "Watch out!" he warned. "Be on your guard against all kinds of greed; a man's life does not consist in the abundance of his possessions."

And he told them this parable: "The ground of a certain rich man produced a good crop. He thought to himself, 'What shall I do? I have no place to store my crops.' Then he said, 'This is what I'll do. I will tear down my barns and build bigger ones, and there I will store all my grain and my goods.'"

At first glance the parable doesn't seem to fit the warning. What's wrong with building bigger barns if the ones you have aren't adequate to contain the crops you've been fortunate enough to harvest? Is that greed or simply need?

What I'm learning about myself is that "greed" and "need" are often interesting bedfellows. For example, I tell myself that I could really use the house in Stanton because, in my little cottage, I've just about run out of room for all my books. And of course I really could use another bedroom for when my many American friends come to visit. The truth is, of course, that my "dream house" in Stanton is so large that it would swallow me alive! I would *never* have enough books to fill it, nor enough guests.

In my saner moments I know that "need" sometimes serves only to mask "greed." After all, what do I really *need*? Each day when I pass by the old village waterspout I am reminded that it wasn't all that long ago that villagers here didn't "need" running water, electricity, or even central sewage. What they didn't have they didn't need. "Need" can be just a smoke-screen for "greed"—a good excuse to have what we want.

Mine is not the greed that we commonly think of: a desire to amass as much money as humanly possible, or to resort to unethical or immoral means in order to acquire wealth, or to covet something that already belongs to someone else, as if I must somehow dispossess them of it.

The particular kind of greed in which I specialize is not *more*, but *better*. I don't need *another* car, only one which really suits my taste. Not *another* house, only the most perfect Cotswold cottage I can find!

Katie Perry—a wonderful 90-year-old treasure to our family—never fails to amuse us at those times when she'd rather forego doing some burdensome household chore. "I've been made for finer things!" she says with a cute little giggle. That's the spirit, Katie! Me, too!

Sometimes I think that the greed of wanting *better* is more insidious than the greed of wanting *more*. Certainly it's more easily rationalized. Far from being the kind of greed that stoops to crass materialistic striving, my kind of greed appeals to a lofty sense of aesthetics—of beauty, of quality, of what God surely would want me to have! Yet if the sin involved in this kind of greed is not the lust for financial gain, it is sin nevertheless—the sin of discontent. Greed is, after all, the opposite of contentment.

Maybe that explains what I have always found to be so curious about Jesus' warning: "Be on your guard against *all kinds of greed*." Did Jesus really mean that there are *many* kinds of greed? If so, then there may be any number of more subtle ways in which you and I are greedy, wholly apart from money or other material things.

Consider, for example, our sometimes inordinate desire for achievement and recognition. Are we simply greedy for attention? Or perhaps it's that seductive desire for a *better* relationship than the one we already have. (Might unfaithfulness in marriage be motivated more out of *greed* than the *lust* which usually gets top billing?) Could it be a lack of contentment—greed—that prompts us to put careers ahead of family, or ourselves ahead of others? Surely, if we could learn to be content, we would never feel threatened by others or fail to recognize where our primary loyalties ought to lie.

Would that you and I, like the apostle Paul, could say, "I know what it is to be in need, and I know what it is to have plenty. I have learned the secret of being content in any and every situation, whether well fed or hungry, whether living in plenty or in want." As it is, we already live in "plenty." When will we learn that "plenty" doesn't have to be "perfect"?

In our discontent and greed, we miss what Jesus wants to teach us about true joy. How could we ever be discontented with things here on earth if we have put our affection on things above? In view of eternity, what is there to really worry about in the here and now?

When we learn "godliness with contentment," we recognize the real folly of greed: It shifts the spotlight away from that which ought to make us happiest. Always wanting more tomorrow keeps us from truly and fully entering into the moment today!

Thinking about a dream house makes you overlook what you like about the house you're already in. Daydreaming about how romantic life might be with someone else makes you forget all the things you first loved about the person you married. Always looking for some other way to be successful robs you of the enjoyment you should experience out of that which you've already achieved.

Those who can't live with godly contentment in the *here and now* will miss out on the joys of even the *there and then*. Heaven itself would disappoint them!

Would that we could be greedy for godliness! For in all other matters we could at last be content. And what a refreshing peace that would bring to our world of constant striving!

Chapter Twelve

"Be kind and
compassionate to
one another."

EPHESIANS 4:32

The Badger

I t was an exciting moment! My first glimpse of a badger! And there was no mistaking it, what with his conspicuous black mask—or "badge"—over his face, and that characteristic stump of a tail. Had it not been in the last shades of twilight, I probably never would have seen him. He comes out only at night, and even then is rarely seen. But here he was, lumbering along ever so slowly, like an old man. As I approached, he quickened his pace and swooshed off into the bushes beyond the nearby gate.

I can relate to the badger's nocturnal habits. When I'm writing, I also sleep in the day and work through the night. However, I'm pleased to say that I do not share his taste in food, which apparently includes beetles, worms, small rodents, and even hedgehogs and rabbits. Using his sharp claws and strong teeth, he digs through the earth to capture his unsuspecting prey. While these skills and physical features earn the badger a comfortable living, unfortunately they've also proved to be the source of great personal danger for him.

The badger has few *natural* enemies, but when did that ever stop *humans* from being a threat? Because of his ability to do serious battle with his intended prey, the badger has been highly sought after for the so-called sport of badger-baiting. Badger-baiting involves putting a badger into either a barrel or a pit specially-dug for the occasion, and then setting vicious dogs on the frightened, normally shy creature. Apparently the fighting is ferocious, with injury to both dogs and badger. But always in the end the badger dies.

Further details aren't necessary. Badger-baiting is heartless and inhumane. We capture but little of its actual brutality in the courtroom objection which takes its name. We lawyers sometimes say of our opponent: "Objection, Your Honor; counsel is *badgering the witness*," meaning that, instead of professionally eliciting testimony, counsel is viciously attacking the witness. And like the badger, the witness is usually helpless in his own defense—caged, as it were, in the witness box and set upon by some overbearing legal beagle!

Frequently we see or hear the phrase "animal cruelty." Almost instinctively we recognize that it means cruelty *against* animals, because the irony is that animals themselves are never cruel. Naturally, animals in the wild do kill, but they kill for food, for the protection of territory, and for family security. And when animals kill, they do so with no known sensitivity toward their victims. There is no mercy in the jungle, no remorse in the deadly waters of the Great Barrier Reef, no "animal rights" on the Serengeti Plain.

Animals may be aggressive, vicious, brutal, deadly, even "mad," but never *cruel*. Never sadistic. Never mean for personal amusement. Never guilty of intentional torture. Cruelty is exclusively a human trait.

But it would be wrong to think, as we typically do, that human cruelty always happens on a grand scale. Cruelty is not found exclusively within the domain of the Holocaust, or such crimes as kidnapping, torture, and rape.

More often, cruelty is my own insensitivity in raising my voice to the inefficient clerk behind the counter. It's my witty yet piercing sarcasm that tears someone's less-confident self-image to shreds. It's my scathing self-righteous censure of others who have no clue about the biblical framework from which I so glibly operate. In so many little ways, human cruelty lurks at my own doorstep.

Why are we that way? What makes those kinds of words come out of our mouths? Somewhere along the line we have missed the message of kindness: "Therefore, as God's chosen people, holy and dearly loved, clothe yourselves with compassion, kindness, humility, gentleness and patience." And "add to your faith...brotherly kindness; and to brotherly kindness, love."

A "kinder and gentler world" is not just a political slogan. Kindness and gentleness are evidence that we have allowed God to work in our relationships with other people. "The fruit of the Spirit," Paul told the Galatians, "is love, joy, peace, patience, kindness, goodness, faithfulness, gentleness and self-control."

Kindness is a godly trait because it mirrors God's own kindness to us. One of the most poignant passages in all of Scripture is found in the prophecy of Hosea, where God pictures the people of Israel as his little children that he lovingly nourished and tenderly cared for:

> It was I who taught Ephraim to walk,
> taking them by the arms;
> but they did not realize
> it was I who healed them.
> I led them with cords of human kindness,
> with ties of love;
> I lifted the yoke from their neck
> and bent down to feed them.

We can learn to tie cords of human kindness instead of tying cords that bind people. Malice can't survive in the presence of compassion. In all his scathing rebukes of the religious leaders of his day, Jesus never once was unkind. He told it like it was, but never did he beat sinners into the ground! Something about how Jesus spoke was so different that even the crowds recognized it.

With Jesus, it wasn't what came out of his *mouth*, but what came out of his *heart*. Where there's a heart filled with love, you'll never find a mouth filled with hate.

Remember that old saying, "Don't kick a man when he's down"? It's our human way of drawing a line at cruelty. It recognizes the virtue of protecting the defenseless. But Jesus' compassion goes much deeper. Jesus always operated at the heart level. He had the ability to always see when a person was "down," and, more importantly, *why* he was "down." Where there was brokenness, Jesus always saw it. And who among us is not broken?

When we turn to God for his leading, we come to recognize the humility of our own brokenness. As we let the Lord's Spirit become active in our lives to heal that brokenness, we realize that other people are hurting too. If cruelty tears down, kindness builds up. Compassion tries to help wherever there is brokenness: to heal the wounds, to forgive the trespasses, to cover over the imperfections we see in others. That is what God himself does. He sees through our sin to our brokenness and then heals, forgives, and covers.

Paraphrasing the apostle John, "We love others because he first loved us!" If God can love us, brokenness and all, we follow his lead in loving others. I think of Peter, who denied Jesus not once but three times. How easy it would have been for Jesus to treat Peter bitterly, to make him feel as small as he had acted. But Jesus didn't say a word. Is that because Jesus understood how easy it is for us to betray even our best intentions when we're overwhelmed by insecurity and fear? Was that the brokenness Jesus saw in Peter?

Someone might suggest that surely there must have been cruelty in Jesus' eyes when "the Lord turned and looked straight at Peter." We all know those "looks that can kill." But Peter's reaction tells a different story. When he saw Jesus looking at him, "Then Peter remembered the word the Lord had spoken to him: 'Before the rooster crows today, you will disown me three times.' And he went outside and wept bitterly."

Had Jesus' glance been a look of cruelty, Peter might never have been salvaged. As likely as not, he would have used that cruelty to justify his own disloyalty. (Why be loyal to someone who isn't big enough to allow for mistakes?) Instead, what Peter saw was a *knowing* look of *disappointment*: disappointment, because love hopes for the very best; knowing, because love recognizes human frailty.

Sometimes we think we can never really emulate Jesus. How can we, being human, ever be so noble, so loving, so compassionate? How can we ensure that we never again give one of those "looks that could kill," or speak the unkind thought?

Perhaps our very humanity can help us in this regard. Every time we look at someone else, we ought to see ourselves, as if in a mirror. Brokenness is brokenness, whether it's in ourselves or in others. Are we unkind to ourselves when we recognize our brokenness? Then why be unkind to others who share our very humanity? We're just broken in different ways, that's all. In love we do unto others what they must do every day unto us in order to put up with our own imperfections!

Isn't that the essence of Jesus' teaching about "doing unto others"?

But I may be wrong to assume that we don't treat our own selves cruelly. Maybe the problem is that we're doing exactly what Jesus told us to do: "Love your neighbor as yourself." If we don't know God's love within our own lives, how can we offer his love to those around us?

That's why it is so important that we learn to accept God's forgiveness of our own sin and brokenness. For God is thereby teaching us how we in turn can forgive the sin and brokenness of those who disappoint *us*.

So what is the spiritual antidote to our temptation to be unkind? One of the best ways of learning compassion is to appreciate that the weakness we see in others—that same weakness that disappoints us, and frustrates us, and angers us to the point of wanting to be unkind in return—*that very weakness* may be a wonderful *strength* under normal circumstances! If we could only know the flip side of the coin, we would lose the drive to be heartless. Knowing their strength, we could compensate more readily for their weakness.

So to the clerk behind the counter whose inefficiency makes me want to throttle him, I need to look as perceptively as Jesus would have looked—to see the flip side, to see the good. Maybe the reason he is so slow is that he is a "people person." Where other clerks couldn't care less about the customers and just get on with their business in a brusque, businesslike fashion, maybe my "inefficient" clerk has a good reason for being slow.

On the other hand, it just may be that my "inefficient" clerk is slow because he's lazy! But if I don't know one way or the other, why not give him the benefit of the doubt? Badgering him is not likely to help, whatever the truth may be. And if I am *right* in thinking that his weakness might really be the flip side of some commendable character trait, then the unkindness I have spared him just might be the encouragement he needs to carry his strength further into his area of weakness.

Isn't that the way God works in our own lives? No one loves us more. And he loves us despite the fact that he knows us inside out. What else can his love mean, then, but that he sees right through our weaknesses to our strengths? God works from his abundance to provide that which is lacking. Instead of rebuking us cruelly, he gives us that "knowing look of disappointment," and calls us higher.

If this is what God does for *us*, how could we not do the same for *others*? We love because he first loved us. How can we continue to be unkind when the Hound of Heaven badgers us with divine acceptance!

Want to have a wonderful day? Try badgering everyone you meet with kindness and compassion!

Chapter Thirteen

"If one falls down,
his friend can
help him up."

ECCLESIASTES 4:10

Walking Stick

I t's just a stick. A plain, ordinary stick of wood. I don't even know what kind of wood it is. Reddish brown and a bit gnarly. Nothing special, really. But this plain, ordinary walking stick has become a constant companion on my daily walks.

The first time I saw the stick, it was leaning next to my woodshed at the side of the cottage. It seemed about the right length, and was sturdy enough. At first it still had all its bark, and the roughness chafed against my hand as I walked. Over several days while rambling in the hills, I carried an old pocket-knife and whittled away the bark. A couple of stubborn knots were eventually shaved down, and it wasn't long before I had myself a piece of wood which seemed tailor-made.

Sometimes I think it's a bit funny to be carrying around a stick. Particularly the one I carry—just a plain ol' stick. It's not as if mine were a *legitimate* walking stick, like the fancy ones sold in all the tourist shops.

I wonder if walking sticks have something to do with memories of our youth. A good strong stick is a child's first weapon and symbol of strength. Those battles against imaginary evil forces in which the stick was wielded ferociously were indeed courageous and brave! Sticks were also handy for terrorizing overgrown backyard territory. Dandelions, tall grass, and menacing bushes were all likely targets for a determined swipe with one's wooden weapon.

So maybe it's a flashback to my youth that prompts me to carry a stick. (I still take an occasional swipe at tall grass and unsuspecting dandelions.) But lately I wonder if it's not just the *old* man in me that insists on carrying a stick. Tall grass on steep slopes is guaranteed complete safety as I trudge breathlessly past, using my stick as a kind of low gear to help me make the grade.

Naturally, I shudder at the thought that my walking stick serves the same purpose as a cane. *Canes* are for doddering old men walking precariously along a level street—somewhat like Zechariah described: "Once again men and women of ripe old age will sit in the streets of Jerusalem, each with cane in hand because of his age."

King David was no "doddering old man" of ripe old age when he found security in the most famous of all walking sticks. But of course the sticks to which he referred were no ordinary sticks. You remember the psalm. It is perhaps the best-known of all the Psalms—the beautiful 23rd. And what could be more appropriate for my own daily walks in the Cotswolds? I too see shepherds, green pastures, quiet waters, paths, and valleys. And so, just as David walked with his "rod and staff," I too carry my trusty stick.

Said David confidently, "Even though I walk through the valley of the shadow of death, I will fear no evil, for you are with me; your rod and your staff, they comfort me." What David carried by faith was the "rod and staff" of God. The *rod*, for David, was a stick of protection against any enemy or threat—a weapon of war, a means of self-defense; the *staff*, on the other hand, was a benign, peaceful walking stick—more like an old friend and faithful companion.

And that is how I see my own walking stick—as both a rod of protection and a staff of friendship. I wouldn't think of leaving it behind whenever I go out for a walk. Maybe I'm desperate for companionship, but there it is, like an old friend, always resting comfortably in my hand. Something would be missing if I didn't take it along.

I don't consciously think about it in advance, but on those rare occasions when a snarling dog lunges at my feet, or one of the stallions in the field gallops headlong in my direction, it's always comforting to know that I've got some protection available just in case I need it. At those times, my "staff" of companionship becomes my "rod" of assurance.

This must be the daily message of my walking stick. Through good times and bad, God is my rod and my staff. He is both my greatest protection and my most faithful friend. It would not be enough for my God to provide only one without the other—either protection without friendship, or friendship without protection.

A God who protects without offering friendship would be a stern, cold, authoritative, and frightening God. The power wielded by such a God would as likely take a swipe at *me* as at my enemies. That's not the kind of God I know, but such a God is how many people interpret the God of the Old Testament.

It's no surprise that we would rather think about the God of the New Testament, as viewed through the Person of Jesus Christ. Who could have been more gentle, loving, and accepting than Jesus? "What a friend we have in Jesus!" declares the hymn, with a sense of great relief. The *rod* of God has been replaced with a *staff*!

But there is danger in thinking that the God of the Bible is Dr. Jekyll and Mr. Hyde, or even in seeing God only as all "sweetness and love." For a God who would offer friendship without providing strength and protection would be a frothy, sentimental, powerless God. Divine friendship alone would be virtually worthless in those times when I need to depend on Someone greater than myself—which is every moment of the day!

The good news is that Jesus is *both* our protector *and* our friend! The apostle Paul prayed that the believers in Ephesus would come to know God better and better, especially "his incomparably great power for us who believe. That power is like the working of his mighty strength, which he exerted in Christ when he raised him from the dead and seated him at his right hand in the heavenly realms...."

Our God is no weakling. Our God is the risen Savior of the world! A God of power over death itself!

Yes, our God is a God of love. But it is a love that *protects* as well as cares. There is no more reassuring passage in all the Bible than Paul's reminder that in Christ "we are more than conquerors through him who loved us." "For I am convinced," says Paul, "that neither death nor life, neither angels nor demons, neither the present nor the future, nor any powers, neither height nor depth, nor anything else in all creation, will be able to separate us from the love of God that is in Christ Jesus our Lord."

God's love is not the soppy sentimentalism that mere friendship might be. God's love is power! God's love is strength! God's love is protection!

Whether it be times of sickness, loneliness, or fear, or even when "I walk through the valley of the shadow of death"—I know that, like David and Paul and a host of God's people who have gone before, "I can do everything through him who gives me strength."

What a joy it is to know that my protector is also my friend. It didn't have to be that way. The idolater, for example, may have his imagined "protector," but he can have no pretense of a friend. The superstitious person believes in magical powers, but magic holds no hands. That's the amazing thing about the incarnation of Jesus—not just God in *heaven*, imbued with power and majesty, but God in *flesh*, seeking fellowship and friendship. *Our* friendship!

As he said to his chosen disciples, Jesus also says to us, "I no longer call you servants, because a servant does not know his master's business. Instead, I have called you friends, for everything that I learned from my Father I have made known to you." *"Friends"* with God? We are actually *friends* with the One who created us? What an amazing and altogether wondrous thought!

Maybe you should consider getting yourself a walking stick. Just put it right there in the corner of your room, whether you have a house in the suburbs or perhaps an apartment in the city. You may never use it in the Cotswolds, but what a graphic reminder of God's power and love it could be. And if anyone should ask, just tell them with a twinkle in your eye that your best Friend and greatest Protector left it there one day.

Chapter Fourteen

"Let us discern for
ourselves what is
right; let us learn
together what
is good."

JOB 34:4

Lambing Time

I love lambing time. All of those little wet and wobbly lambs coming fresh into the world, shaking their heads and taking those first wondrous steps. It's a magical time in the Cotswolds. Actually, it is a *miraculous* time. How it all happens still amazes me. For the Buckland families who raise sheep, it means long nights and hard work. For me, the spectator, it's simply great joy!

In his *Farmer's Diary*, shepherd R.W.F. Poole describes the first few days after the lambing takes place. Early on, the time is spent "mothering up," as shepherds call it. (We would call it "maternal bonding.") It's all about getting the baby to love its mother and vice versa. Normally all goes well—probably better than with humans. But invariably there are a few "problem mothers" who try to kick their lambs out of the pen, or give them a good head-butting.

The answer, says Poole, is to clamp the mother's neck in a yoke, so that the lambs can suckle unmolested. The ewe is kept that way until her maternal instincts have rallied a bit, then she's released from the yoke and there begins a gradual process of increasing the size of the mothering groups as the success of the bonding improves. Usually by the end of a week, mother and offspring are inseparable.

That's where I come in. Enter stranger, over the stile and into the field, and the pasture immediately becomes a mass of trotting mothers blaring for their lambs. Usually it's the Noah Principle—calling them two by two! And here they come rushing. That's when the truly amazing matching-up process takes place.

It doesn't matter if there are a hundred other ewes in the field, the lambs run right past them to their own mothers and quickly begin to suckle. Two at a time, the lambs go for the mother's teats with such force that it lifts her back feet off the ground. As much a matter of security as feeding, the mother lets her lambs know that they are all right, and then walks ahead of them, leading them out of harm's way.

But how does the matching-up process work? Is it like a human mother who, with one look, can pick out her own child from among a whole nursery full of squalling newborns? From what I'm told, with lambs it's not a matter of sight, but sound. That's what all that raucous blaring is about. Although to my ear one "baaah" sounds pretty much like another "baaah," apparently the lamb recognizes its mother's distinctive voice. The "mothering up" process is good not only for feeding but also for making permanent voiceprint impressions.

Of course, there is yet another voice that sheep come to recognize—the voice of the shepherd. Perhaps that too is due to a certain "mothering up" process resulting from the feeding and sense of security which the shepherd provides. Should it be any surprise, then, that we have a spiritual parallel in Jesus?

Said Jesus, "The man who enters by the gate is the shepherd of his sheep. The watchman opens the gate for him, and the sheep listen to his voice. He calls his own sheep by name and leads them out. When he has brought out all his own, he goes on ahead of them, and his sheep follow him because they know his voice."

Jesus, of course, is the perfect, the quintessential Shepherd. At first not even his disciples understood this. So he said to them again, "I am the good shepherd; I know my sheep and my sheep know me—just as the Father knows me and I know the Father—and I lay down my life for the sheep."

How do the sheep know the shepherd? By his *voice*, says Jesus.

As I think about my own father, one of the things I remember most about him is the sound of his voice. How could I ever forget its many tones—sometimes gentle, when I was troubled and scared; sometimes demanding, perhaps when I was too slow in getting out of bed.

But there is a more insightful way that I know my father, even though I can no longer hear his voice. I know him in the closeness of the relationship we shared, and in my familiarity with his inner being. I know how he thought. I know what he believed. I know what he stood for.

Surely that is what Jesus meant when he said that his sheep know his voice. As Jesus' disciples—as his *sheep*—we don't literally hear Jesus talking to us. Jesus' voice hasn't been heard on earth since the first century. But as Christians we have a relationship with the Good Shepherd that permits us to know his inner being. As people of faith, we know how he thinks. We know what he believes. We know what he stands for.

Almost as important as recognizing the voice of the Good Shepherd is the ability to recognize when it is *not* his voice calling us. Even lambs don't follow the call of a stranger. In fact they run headlong *away* from strangers—back to the one voice they can depend on! This was Jesus' very point. His sheep hear his voice and follow him, he said, "but they will never follow a stranger; in fact, they will run away from him because they do not recognize a stranger's voice."

Whose voice are *we* listening to? Do we act as if there are no enemies prowling about—no need to stay near to him who protects us? Are we listening to voices that would lure us away from his care? Voices that seem more exciting, more sophisticated?

Indeed, have we begun to listen to *our own* voice? Do we dream our own dreams and attribute them to the voice of God? Do we read into Scripture what we want to find? Have we begun to say, "God said to me..." even when it may run counter to a clear biblical teaching? What a tragedy it would be if we ourselves became the "stranger" among God's sheep!

Like sheep, the only way to truly know the voice of God is to make sure that we have gone through the process of "mothering up." Without our own spiritual commitment to obediently follow God's leading, even the Scriptures can be the instrument of counterfeit voices.

Hearing God's voice is principally a matter of spiritual discernment. "The man without the Spirit," says Paul, "does not accept the things that come from the Spirit of God, for they are foolishness to him, and he cannot understand them, because they are spiritually discerned."

As human beings born of flesh, we are like wet and wobbly little lambs before the "mothering up" process. Through our strictly human ears, hearing God's voice is not always easy. But as believers born of the Spirit, we are able to discern, not only the voice of the Good Shepherd, but the counterfeit voices of "strangers" who would seek to lead us astray.

What intrigues me most about the little lambs running for their mothers at the first hint of danger is their immediate urge to suckle. Even for little lambs, a sense of security is automatically associated with their dependence upon that which gives sustenance. Instinctively they know the source of their own life, and it is to that source that they run.

How sad it is that we too often turn to God only when something frightening happens to us. At those times, if at no other, we recognize our complete dependence upon God for our very survival. If only we could realize how absolutely essential it is that we turn to God *daily*, aware that there is simply nowhere else to go. That there is no other worthy explanation, no other encouragement, no other hope. That he alone is the One who leads us out of harm's way.

Wouldn't it be wonderful if we could begin each day recognizing our great need for spiritual nourishment and strength, and praising him for being the true source of our life, the One in whose image we want to be continually re-created.

The more we come to know God, the more we appreciate how very much he desires to satisfy our hearts with their every longing and need. Nothing is too much for us to ask. Certainly he is our Source, but even more, he is our Sustainer. He suckles us with life and love!

If wet and wobbly little lambs are lovable because they are so dependent and vulnerable, how much more lovable we must be in the heart of God! That thought alone ought to send us running to his open arms. And he isn't hard to find. Just listen to his voice. Over and over he calls to us.

Chapter Fifteen

"What good is it
for a man to gain
the whole world, yet
forfeit his soul?"

MARK 8:36

The Rectory

Not a day goes by that I don't cast a passing glance at the old two-story rectory, sitting sadly unoccupied in run-down gardens. At first glance, much about the building itself looks normal. Once touted as the longest continuously occupied rectory in all of England—over 450 years—it was home to a succession of local church officials following its initial occupancy. Originally built in the early 1400s, the grand house boasts of medieval, open-timbered rafters and spacious, high-ceiling rooms on either side of a great hall. Its stately presence defies you to walk by without noticing it.

But the rectory has been left empty and neglected for over five years now. Oh, there's no concern about it deteriorating anytime soon. It's been standing with dignity for centuries and is not likely to give up easily at this point. But it's somewhat like the "whitewashed tombs" of which Jesus spoke: structurally sound on the outside, but with signs of disrepair within. The once-magnificent old rectory stares in blank silence at all who pass by, as if robbed of its very soul.

The rectory is like a lot of people—functioning normally on the outside, but lifeless within. It might be people we would least suspect—perhaps even some of the most "successful" people we know. On the job, they may be people we look up to and admire for their gift of organization, yet their private lives might be in utter chaos. In the workplace, we may envy the exuberant confidence that sees them through any crisis. Yet within themselves, night after sleepless night, they may experience an excruciating crisis in confidence.

What is it that destroys the inner person? That decays the soul and leaves a void where once there was vitality, self-assurance, and motivation? If the rectory is any clue, perhaps it is the absence of purpose. The rectory is not meant to be simply a *house*, but a *home*. It's meant for life, love, and laughter. Without those things, it's just an empty shell. It might as well be a barn. No, for even a barn, if it is still in use, serves a higher purpose than a house that is not a home.

As with the rectory, so it is with each of us. Each of us needs a reason to go on—some special purpose within ourselves that prompts our daily actions and pushes us forward. What we need is meaning in our lives. What we need is an understanding of who we are, where we've come from, where we're going. Without a vision, the people perish!

In this day and age, most of us have been taught to believe that we are the purposeless product of blind chance operating in a haphazard universe, with neither a soul nor a future destiny. What meaning can there possibly be in such a scenario? What does such a story give anyone to believe in? Am I truly to live my life assuming at the deepest level that there is no inherent purpose for my existence?

What evolutionary theory takes away from man, modern psychology attempts to restore. But because much of modern psychology assumes our supposed haphazard appearance on the earth, it attempts that task in vain. A psychology denying that man was purposely made in the image of God takes away the human soul. And man without a soul is an empty house. Man without a soul knows little of life, love, and laughter. Where, without a soul, is the joy? Where the hope? Where the sense of direction which keeps a person going?

I might feel better about the rectory if someone at least cleaned up the place and painted it—and better still if someone furnished it with wonderful period pieces that restored its former beauty. Yet such a flurry of activity reminds me of what we often do to fill the aching void in our own lives.

We spend much of our time and effort "fixing up the place." Travel, entertainment, education, and sports all help to pass the time. Our maddening pace distracts us from the emptiness that threatens, moment by moment, to suck us into its black hole of meaningless existence.

But none of this manufactured, frenzied activity can truly bring meaning into lives, any more than a fresh coat of paint and roomfuls of furniture could truly restore the rectory. Just check out the latest list of those who have committed suicide, and you will see people who had managed to accumulate all there was to accumulate, to experience all there was to experience, and to learn all that the human mind could possibly know. Still, they found life not worth living.

"To be, or not to be?" is not the only question. "*Why* to be?" is the question that really counts. Not knowing *why* we exist is the reason for too many deciding "*not* to be."

Never has the search for meaning been more clearly articulated than in King Solomon's Ecclesiastes. However, if the reader is not careful, it might appear that Solomon was convinced that his life was without purpose. "Vanity of vanities, all is vanity," lamented this wisest of all men. "'Meaningless! Meaningless!' says the Teacher. 'Everything is meaningless!'"

But look carefully at what he found to be meaningless: achievement, labor, accumulation, wealth, materialism, prosperity, power, even wisdom. Why did Solomon consider these things which we pursue so relentlessly to be meaningless?

Because we can't take any of them with us when we die. And die we must. "All come from dust, and to dust all return," is Solomon's sobering reminder.

This is not to say that life isn't worth living for its own sake. Again and again, Solomon urges us to live life with gusto—to eat our food with gladness, to drink with a joyful heart, to "enjoy life with your wife, whom you love."

How then would Solomon see both the big picture and the significance of our day-to-day living? "Remember your Creator in the days of your youth," he urges. Acknowledging that we are part of a purposeful creation is the first and most important step in making sense of life. It assures us that we didn't just happen by chance—struggling to make it through "survival of the fittest" or whatever other rule of the jungle man might define. It tells us that we are here for a reason—to have a dynamic relationship with the One who made us.

With purpose comes a sense of calling and a recognition of our giftedness. If we have a specific purpose in life, surely we are specially equipped for the task ahead. "For we are God's workmanship, created in Christ Jesus to do good works, which God prepared in advance for us to do," says the apostle Paul. God is not sorry he made you. He has plans!

Solomon then reminds us that there is more to us than mind and body, both of which will see decay. It's not *just* dust to dust. "The dust returns to the ground it came from, and the spirit returns to God who gave it." "Then," says Solomon, "man goes to his eternal home." We are mind, body, *and* spirit. And destined for eternity!

With that grand thought we are taken beyond the material world into the sublime. To a new appreciation of *meaning*, God also adds *hope*. For those who come to understand their true purpose in living, life has meaning even beyond the grave. More than simply understanding what *this* life is all about, we have been given a hunger for our *eternal home!*

With heaven awaiting us, death is no longer the end. Nor is it to be feared. Because of Christ's own sacrificial death and glorious resurrection, we can join Paul in saying confidently, "Where, O death, is your victory? Where, O death, is your sting?" In Christ, the faithful will live forever!

Yet Solomon ends on a somber tone, for much is at stake in the pursuit of meaning. "Now all has been heard," says the wise man; "here is the conclusion of the matter: Fear God and keep his commandments, for this is the *whole* of man. For God will bring every deed into judgment, including every hidden thing, whether it is good or evil." Did that ruin the pretty picture of a refurbished rectory filled with life, love, and laughter? Did someone open a door, letting in a chilling gust of wind?

I for one often need a wintry blast to wake me up and remind me that my life is lived before the God who made me—that his world does not revolve around me, but that my life finds its meaning in *him*. No, living in fear is not my purpose in life; but I do fear missing out on life's purpose! And I fear the awful emptiness in the words which Jesus said to those who had rejected him: "Look, your house is left to you desolate."

What's really happening in my life? Am I a *house* or a *home*? Am I wasting a lifetime decorating my mind and body while ignoring the soul, which is the only part of me that will live beyond the grave? If I've decided my life is "to *be*," have I given it a reason to know *why* it's to be?

Some awfully nice folks have bought the rectory now and are making every effort to restore it to its former glory. I can't wait until they move in! I want to see the grand hall once again lighted at night, perhaps for a special dinner or birthday party. And won't it be fun when the grandchildren come for a visit, and when aunts and uncles and cherished friends drop by? Already it's a grand house. Just imagine what a wonderful *home* it will be!

If you've ever felt that your life is empty and without purpose, you should know that God has something special in mind for you. He wants there to be lights in your eyes and happiness in your heart. He's throwing a party just for you! All you've got to do is to let him move in and fill your life.

If you don't feel very special or beautiful, just wait until he starts redecorating! God doesn't care about how attractive we might be on the outside. Anyone can put on a coat of paint to cover up the weathering of passing years, but the believer has a greater promise: The Bible says that those who have come to God are clothed with his own righteousness. Having surrounded us with divine beauty, God looks on the inside and knows how truly beautiful you can be—and already are!

That's why Jesus is always at the door of our hearts, waiting to come in. He's more than a friend dropping by for a visit; he's there to make your house his home. Let him be more and more at home in your heart, and there'll be no end to life, love, and laughter!

Chapter Sixteen

"We who have
believed enter
that rest."

HEBREWS 4:3

INVITATION

Gates

Some open, some shut. Some fancy, some plain. When walking through the Cotswolds, one can expect to find any number of gates along the way. That's because there are so many fences, designed either to keep animals in or intruders out. But if fences are barriers, gates are invitations. If fences say "No Trespassing," gates say "Welcome." Like old friends, gates along the footpaths give unspoken permission to "come along and enjoy yourself."

In the English countryside, even the simplest gate seems to have its own special character. Often there's something decorative or ornate about the gate. And because gates are like invitations, it's no more than one might expect. What wedding or party invitation isn't beautifully embellished?

One of the grandest gates in these parts is the gate leading to the manor house in Stanway. There the three-story ornate stone gate is itself an entire house. And so beautiful is this gatehouse that photographs of it adorn virtually every picture book of the Cotswolds.

The many gates which I encounter during my daily walks here in the Cotswolds help to bring into clearer perspective the reason why Jesus once described himself as a gate. "I am the gate," he told his listeners. "Whoever enters through me will be saved." As a gate, Jesus invites us to enter into a new relationship with God. If there are obstacles standing in the way—whether nagging doubts and disbeliefs or perhaps our own stubborn pride—Jesus is the gate by which we gain access to God.

To us, Jesus himself extends beautifully embellished invitations. *Welcomed* invitations like, "Come to me, all you who are weary and burdened, and I will give you rest." *Wedding* invitations like, "The Spirit and the bride say, 'Come!'...Whoever is thirsty, let him come; and whoever wishes, let him take the free gift of the water of life." With invitations like these, who could refuse to accept!

Yet I am intrigued by the context in which Jesus described himself as a gate. Appropriately enough for the Cotswolds, it has to do with being the gate to a sheep pen.

"I tell you the truth," said Jesus, "the man who does not enter the sheep pen by the gate, but climbs in by some other way, is a thief and a robber....I am the gate; whoever enters through me will be saved. He will come in and go out, and find pasture. The thief comes only to steal and kill and destroy; I have come that they may have life, and have it to the full."

When Jesus said that he was "the gate," he was offering a beautifully embellished invitation to "come in and go out, and find pasture." He was also warning his hearers that he was *the* gate to the sheep pen—that is, there is only *one* gate! As the exclusive way to spiritual happiness, Jesus is both the divine "welcome" sign and a sober reminder that trying to find lasting fulfillment along any other path is futile.

If Jesus was *not* God, as he claimed to be, then all roads might indeed lead to heaven, and any gate would do. But if Jesus was telling the truth about being God, then he alone is the One through whom the world was made, the One who knows us better than we know ourselves, and the One who knows the path to spiritual life.

The more I observe the sheep around me in the fields, the more I am beginning to appreciate the image of Jesus being an *exclusive* gate. Sheep are hardly expert at distinguishing between fences and gates. Try to direct a truant sheep back into the proper field through an open gate and you're likely to find that the sheep will prefer to make its own way—even, if necessary, through a barbed-wire fence!

I don't know about you, but I identify a lot more with that truant sheep than I usually want to admit! Every time I turn around, I find myself wondering why things aren't going right for me.

At times, when I finally wake up to how foolish I've been and how much trouble it's gotten me into, I think of that prodigal son whom Jesus told about—the son who did what he thought was the natural thing to do: to take his inheritance early and set out to make his fortune. Of course, we know what happened along the glittering road to success. The son squandered all his money and ended up feeding the pigs!

The happiness and fulfillment he thought he would find turned out to be sheer illusion. He would have been better off working for his father—someone who would understand his dreams and love him enough to give him anything he might truly need.

When this "prodigal son" finally admitted to himself how truly lost he was, he was ready to learn the most important lesson of all—that fulfillment rarely comes to us when it is our only goal. If we can ever get over our stubborn insistence on doing it *our* way, we just might find the happiness that eludes us. Nothing could be more inviting than the words written on the heavenly gate: "I have come that they may have life, and have it to the full."

What this young man did in the end was what each of us must do: lay down our pride, get out of the muck of our stifling self-determination, and find our way back to God through the true gate to spiritual fulfillment. When the "lost son" returned to his home, his father welcomed him with open arms and celebration. The happiness that the son was searching for in his life had been there all along, right in front of his eyes!

What I like about the majestic gatehouse at Stanton is the expectation it stirs. If someone has gone to this much trouble just to build a *gate*, imagine what must await us on the inside! An embellished gate is only a foretaste of what is yet to come. It's an invitation to something far grander. And in the case of the palatial manor house at Stanton, that expectation is proved true. It is grand beyond belief!

On a much more majestic scale, of course, it makes me think of Jesus saying to his disciples, "In my Father's house are many rooms; if it were not so, I would have told you. I am going there to prepare a place for you." The manor house at Stanton makes one appreciate all the more Jesus' picture of heaven as a palatial mansion, grander than grand! How could one possibly describe it?

In its heyday, the manor house must have been a flurry of activity, with dinner parties and wonderful events of all sorts. Can't you just imagine lords and ladies and even members of the royal family, all decked out in their finest regalia, gathering for some special occasion? With the most important people being invited, surely every occasion was a gala celebration!

Of course, that is what made each occasion so special: It was an honor and privilege simply to be on the guest list. Then to be driven in a stately carriage through that beautiful gate, and up the path to the manor house, must have really been a thrill!

But if that scene captures your imagination, it doesn't even begin to compare with the glories of heaven. Paul borrows from the prophet Isaiah to paint this wonderful picture for us: "As it is written: 'No eye has seen, no ear has heard, no mind has conceived what God has prepared for those who love him.'" Heaven is not about harps and wings and golden streets. Heaven is about celebration, and praise, and relationship with God!

The apostle John, there on that ancient Isle of Patmos, shared with us this vision of heaven given by Jesus himself: "Then I saw a new heaven and a new earth, for the first heaven and the first earth had passed away....And I heard a loud voice from the throne saying, 'Now the dwelling of God is with men, and he will live with them. They will be his people, and God himself will be with them and be their God. He will wipe every tear from their eyes. There will be no more death or mourning or crying or pain, for the old order of things has passed away.' He who was seated on the throne said, 'I am making everything new!'"

What a glorious place heaven will be! A *spiritual* mansion, with each person there being a special guest of honor. And what a promise: "I am making everything new!" But the surprise is that when Paul talked about eyes not having seen and ears not having heard what God has prepared for us, he wasn't talking directly about heaven. Whatever it is that God has prepared for us, Paul tells us that "God has revealed it to us by his Spirit." The relationship God desires to share with us is for *this* life, as well as for our eternal home. For the faithful, heaven can't wait!

Ever wish you could start over? Do you wish you could bring freshness and renewal into your marriage, or come to terms with your neighbor, or receive God's forgiveness for the sin in your life? Have you ever wanted to throw off your drab past, get dressed up, and go to a party? The bad news is that we can never hope to find that kind of renewal on our own. No party we could ever throw could possibly satisfy our deepest longings.

But the good news is that a celebration has already been planned in your honor! It's a celebration of new beginnings, and the guest list is a virtual "Who's Who" of honorees who were also given new beginnings. King David will be there, and the sinful woman who anointed Jesus' feet. Also Rahab the harlot and Peter and Miriam and Paul. And don't forget all the prodigal sons who have ever returned to seek their Father's face. They will all be there as well.

The invitation is yours. God wants you to have life and *have it to the full*! Right now. Today.

Come to the celebration; everyone is anxious for your arrival. The other guests don't want to go in before you do, so don't disappoint them. They're waiting for you with great anticipation—just inside the Gate.

Chapter Seventeen

"Love your enemies,
do good to those
who hate you."

LUKE 6:27

The Sheep

Walking in the Cotswolds on a summer's eve is a wide-awake, dreamy slumber of the soul! Serene. Carefree. Soft. At one of my favorite spots I sometimes take a break from my walking to sit down and absorb the ambience. This particular spot is best enjoyed at the end of a long June or July day, when not even the setting sun will bring on the final darkness of night. Summer nights in England last forever!

Across several fields to my right, the sun's dying brilliance sets fire to the mullioned windows of the dining hall in the manor house. On the front lawn is a towering, absolutely majestic copper beech tree, resplendently decked out in its deep-toned summer frock.

Nearer to where I sit are the ever-present sheep. Except for the occasional cries of hungry lambs in search of their mothers' milk, they too are quietly grazing. The sheep in this field always seem unusually curious about my daily walks among them. Sometimes they nudge ever so closely in my direction, curious as to what kind of creature I am.

I return their curiosity, wondering what goes on in their minds as they chew the grass in a never-ending pursuit of eating. I wonder if they ever luxuriate in the warmth of a summer's eve, or appreciate the beauty of the setting sun reflected in the manor house windows, or consider the majesty of the towering copper beech.

In another century, the English poet William Blake—whom I could imagine sitting on this very spot—asked a deeper question: "Little Lamb, who made thee? Dost thou know who made thee?" Blake's poem goes on to assume that the little lamb is not, in fact, conscious of his Creator.

Unlike us, neither sheep, nor cows, nor horses—nor any other bird, fish, or insect—was created in the image of God. Unlike us, animals do not contemplate life, or appreciate the aesthetic beauty of nature, or experience the range of moral feelings from guilt to forgiveness. Animals may respond to discipline and approval, but they know nothing of the moral dimension related to the human heart.

Can you imagine what it would be like to be an animal, without any history of the past or hope for the future? Or what it would be like to lack the human traits we take for granted? Love, for example—what does a sheep know of love? I see the ewes being instinctively protective of their young, but neither love nor marriage (nor, for that matter, hatred or estrangement) appear to be part of a sheep's existence.

In a world increasingly bent on reducing the distance between man and animals, it is easy to forget just how far distanced we really are, and therefore how specially blessed!

One of the most intriguing passages in all of Scripture helps to better define the way in which we are uniquely "made in the image of God." Remember when God brought the beasts of the field and the birds of the air before Adam so that he could name them? The point of the exercise was to show that no creature was suitable as a partner for Adam because no other creature—whether beast, fish, or fowl—is on a par with man. No animal comes close—not even "man's best friend"!

The fact that Eve was created, in Adam's words, as "bone of my bones and flesh of my flesh," confirmed in the grandest possible way that human beings, both male and female, are sublimely different from the rest of God's creation. Different not only by *degree* (as in some upwardly evolving progression), but in *kind*.

Being made "in God's image" means that we have a unique capacity for moral reflection and choice, a unique sense of aesthetics, and a unique ability to love.

What I find interesting about our uniqueness is the parallel between each of those special human traits: moral choice, aesthetic appreciation, and the ability to love. If we have one, we have them all; they come as a package. Whereas animals have none of those traits, no man or woman is without them. It might all be sheer coincidence, were it not for the practical way in which our being created "in the image of God" helps us to reflect God's image in a far deeper, more spiritual sense.

Take the matter of love, for example. Scripture tells us to "love one another" and to "love your neighbor as yourself." It even tells us to "love your enemies." All of these are very much a matter of Christian obedience. But how do we *do* that? How, in particular, can we ever come to love our *enemies*?

Tough love was the lesson that Jesus taught again and again to his disciples. Not only did he command, "Love your enemies," but he also gave the incredible command, "Do good to them, and lend to them without expecting to get anything back!"

"Give to our *enemies*, Lord?" they must have asked. "Surely no one can be expected to love his enemies!" But back came Jesus' reply: "If you love those who love you, what credit is that to you?" Loving the lovable is *easy* love. It's loving the unlovable that stretches the nature of who we are.

For me, learning that kind of love has seemed at times as impossible as teaching a sheep to love! It defies logic. Oh, I can restrain myself from actually doing some kind of harm to my enemy. But don't ask me to *love* him! After all, if he were actually lovable, then he wouldn't be my enemy in the first place, would he?

And yet somehow, some way, it *must* be possible, because Jesus said of his own enemies, "Father, forgive them, for they do not know what they are doing." Therefore, as a follower of Jesus, God's same grace must also be working in me to make tough love possible.

The more I think about it, the more I'm convinced that it goes back to those soft summer evenings and the towering copper beech. What's impossible for a sheep to appreciate is easy for me to appreciate, because the Creator of all nature has made me "in his own image." How then could I *not* appreciate the beauties of his creation?

And for the very same reason I should be able to love in extraordinary ways. Did we not say that a sense of aesthetics and a capacity to love come as a package deal—that if you have one you have the other? Surely those parallel traits provide the key to loving where love is difficult.

Have you ever considered that tough love is made easier when we use our God-given sense of aesthetics to help us see beauty in the midst of human frailty? It helps us love others by looking beyond their hostility to their motives—to the hearts of those who are honestly trying to do what is right *as they see it*. It also gives us more compassion for the life-changing events that influence the decisions people make.

Could it be that Jesus was able to reach out to those who tormented him because he saw beauty in people who had been touched by many of life's cruelties? If Jesus could love those who crucified the Son of God, who is there that *we* cannot love? By the grace of God tough love is possible once I have experienced his unconditional love for me. His love strengthens me to look for the beauty in my enemies.

All of us are a mixture; in each of us there is good and bad. From our perspective, of course, an enemy exhibits much more bad than good. But there is always the good, always the beautiful, always something that can be salvaged.

I've done some hard thinking recently about hard loving. I've tried to look into the hearts of those who despise and abuse me, those who have betrayed me and those who hold me in ridicule. I don't know that I'll ever put them at the top of my list of friends, or add them to my social calendar, but my attitude toward them has changed.

I've begun to look for the beauty in those who treat me poorly, and to my great surprise, I've found it! There are those whose personal perspective is strangely skewed, but whose motives are pure. There are others whose ugliness to me seems to reflect events in their lives which, had they happened to me, might also have affected my decisions in life.

If I still have difficulty loving the unlovable in my enemies, at least I have learned to love that which *is* lovable in them. Looking for what beauty there is has made *impossible* love become *possible*. In a few cases, I've even found that the beauty outweighs the ugliness, and have loved my enemies into loving me in return. Looking for the beauty has chased hatred away and brought renewed friendships.

I wish the sheep looking at me with such curious gazes could somehow sense the beauty of our surroundings. Soft summer evenings and towering copper beeches deserve to be noticed! But I wouldn't wish for the sheep a sense of aesthetic appreciation if it also meant their having to know hatred.

Why then should I want any less for myself? I was created for greater things than hatred. I was made for beauty; I was made for love. Even *tough* love, if need be.

Chapter Eighteen

"The Lord turns
my darkness
into light."

2 SAMUEL 22:29

Darkness

L ittle did I suspect how the day would end. I had set out one evening on my walk to Stanton, normally about an hour's round-trip from the cottage. That should have given me enough time to complete the circuit just as darkness would be settling in. As I headed up the village lane, I stopped for a while to talk to Mick and Nan Clarke, who were out working in their picture-perfect garden at the front of their picture-perfect cottage, Tumbledown.

Realizing that it was getting late, I excused myself and walked on up into the hills. Crossing behind the manor house, I climbed over the fence into the next field. As I headed up toward the gate to the field beyond, I met a newcomer to the neighboring village of Laverton. Time passed quickly as we exchanged greetings and got acquainted.

When we finally left in different directions, it wasn't long before I realized how dark it had gotten. In truth, I was more than a little concerned. Could I make it all the way to Stanton and back before the last of the twilight was gone? Already, a cold gloomy mist was moving in over the hills.

Over fence and field, I hurried my pace as if racing with myself. Except for the rustling of treetops, as birds would suddenly fly away upon hearing my hurried approach, it was strangely quiet. It seemed as if every living creature had already bedded down for the night.

By the time I reached Stanton, the sky had gone completely dark, and not a glimmer of moon was to be seen. I could hardly make out the first gate heading me homeward, but I launched determinedly out into the darkness. First one field, then another. A familiar fence, a familiar gate, a familiar path. Onward I went in complete darkness.

I began to wonder what it would be like for anyone else trying to grope his way along. Only my intimate familiarity with the path made it possible for me to keep going. Where others would have been hopelessly lost in the darkness, familiarity was my light.

As I slowly made my way, almost by instinct, I couldn't help but think of the words of the psalm, "Your Word is a lamp to my feet and a light for my path." In the deep darkness of that night, I was able to see more clearly than ever just how God's revelation works in my life. The Bible is not simply the story of human existence, but that upon which I can depend in times of trouble. It is the light in my darkened world of "lostness." No matter how adverse the circumstances, somehow it always gets me through.

For me, the Bible is neither a fail-safe mantra to be recited at the first alarm, nor a tag-along security blanket to ward off all potential enemies. Rather, it has become as familiar as the path to and from my home—so familiar, in fact, that I often fail to appreciate it fully until I find myself in some kind of trouble. But it is precisely in those special times of need that his Word becomes my light, showing the way to safety.

More and more, I am beginning to see the very practical way in which Scripture sheds light on the true path, the true way—or, put simply, *the truth*. Truth that can set me free from worry and fear. Truth that I can depend on, rather than groping along in anxious darkness.

On that dark night I kept thinking how fearful anyone else might have been if caught out there alone. Yet for me the psalmist puts it perfectly: "The Lord is my light and my salvation—whom shall I fear?" If I can *see* the path, what is there to fear?

The skeptic might point out that I only see the path *by faith*—in my mind's eye. But that is the beauty of God's Word. It is not only written on the pages of the Bible, but in the inner recesses of my heart, stored there for whenever I need to hear the Lord's guidance. In times of spiritual darkness—whether I am confronted with temptation, haunted by fear, or overwhelmed by loneliness—I am better able to find my way out of it. It's almost instinctive, *as if I could actually see the way*. Wherever I am, whatever the need, because of God's Word which is now a part of my very essence, I am always in the grip of the familiar.

In some ways this reminds me of the struggling days and months immediately following the death of my father. There were times when I desperately wanted to pick up the phone and ask Dad's advice on one thing or another, but that was not possible. Even so, I kept having the feeling that, if I had been able to ask him, I knew exactly what Dad would tell me. In fact, I knew my father so well that I could almost hear the very words coming out of his mouth!

Of course, there is an important difference between my earthly father and my heavenly Father. My heavenly Father's voice is not just a memory. Through his Word and through his Spirit, he speaks to me every day. He is literally with me at every moment. Never am I without his involvement in my life. Far greater even than being in the grip of the familiar, I am in *his* grip!

It must be similar to what King David felt when he wrote in his exquisite 23rd Psalm: "Even though I walk through the valley of the shadow of death, I will fear no evil, for you are with me." Not even the anticipated darkness of his own death was fearful for David, for throughout his life he had walked with God on familiar paths. With God constantly in his life, through good times and bad, he lived confidently in the living presence of his Lord.

There must have been nights when, as a shepherd boy, David found himself walking across fields in darkness. Little wonder that he should write in yet another psalm, "If I say, 'Surely the darkness will hide me and the light become night around me,' even the darkness will not be dark to you; the night will shine like the day, for darkness is as light to you." Was it dark nights in the fields or dark nights in the despair of great sin that David had in mind? Perhaps both. Perhaps dark nights alone in the fields had prepared him for even darker nights of moral despair.

When all is said and done, it's all about trusting God in the darkness, whatever the darkness may be. Certainly David would have expected nothing less from him who first made light out of darkness—from him who first said, "Let there be light," and there *was* light!

If God could bring physical light itself into existence, why should I ever think that he could not shed his spiritual light whenever and wherever I might need it? Light to show the way when I am stranded in despair and lost in loneliness. Light to lead me in the paths of right living. And, in the end, light to lead me safely home.

Chapter Nineteen

"The Sabbath was
made for man,
not man for
the Sabbath."

MARK 2:27

Holiday Cottages

Being in Buckland must be heavenly for people from the larger cities of Birmingham, Blackpool, and Bath. Step out of the world of polluting buses, traffic jams, and inner-city noise into a quiet village consisting of only 23 cottages, and life becomes fresh and new.

I see that look of discovery in the eyes of village visitors who come here to kick back and let the rest of the world rush by. It's like a heavy load lifted, or like bandages removed from one's eyes after restorative surgery. One emerges from the "Buckland experience" relaxed and renewed.

In addition to the Buckland Manor, with its mainly upscale guests, we also have a number of what the British refer to as self-catering holiday cottages in the village. The Buckland Court cottages are nestled together in a picturesque group of structures (reminiscent of a little hamlet), all of which are converted farm buildings—grain stores, stables, wagon sheds. "Even the dairy, where once farmhouse butter and cheese were made, has now been charmingly refurbished as the Round House, with honeymoons and romantic breaks in mind," says the brochure.

Just up the lane are Charles Edmondson's two comfortable cottages, with their commanding views across the hills, and the added bonus of an indoor swimming pool behind the red door in the old barn. And hardly a week goes by that Mrs. Knight's charming guest cottage across from the church isn't occupied.

Self-catering is a way of life in rural England. You get your own cottage for a week—complete with linens, dishes, games for the children, and a variety of other holiday extras. Cook for yourself, or dine out in local pubs. Slow down. Take it easy. The Cotswolds are ideal for an English holiday. And the proper word here is *holiday*.

For all its modern equivalent to America's *vacation*, I prefer the British use of "holiday." Trace the word to its origins and you'll discover that it has something to do with *holy* days—like Jewish Passovers, Jubilees, and Sabbaths.

Unlike days, months, and years—all of which relate to some astronomical phenomenon—our seven-day week has no astronomical origin. And yet it is observed in virtually every society throughout the globe. The seven-day week is, in fact, a lasting monument to God's creation of the world. For when God blessed his creation, he included a day of rest and made it *holy*. It was God who first came up with the idea of taking a "holiday."

But God's day of rest was not simply "a day off." God specially consecrated that day as being a "holy" day. It set the stage for what was to become the Jewish day of worship, the Sabbath. What the Jews were told about the Sabbath says much to us also about the holiness of our own "day off." Hear again these powerful words from Deuteronomy:

> Observe the Sabbath day by keeping it
> holy, as the Lord your God has
> commanded you. Six days you shall labor

*and do all your work, but the seventh day
is a Sabbath to the Lord your God. On
it you shall not do any work....Remember
that you were slaves in Egypt and that the
Lord your God brought you out of there with
a mighty hand and an outstretched arm.
Therefore the Lord your God has
commanded you to observe the Sabbath day.*

Resting would be sufficient justification for "a day off," but *remembering* was what made the day *holy*. Remembering what God had done! For the Israelites, the seventh day was to be a back-to-God day in remembrance of his having delivered them from Egyptian bondage. For Christians, the day of remembrance would change to the first day of the week, because it was on the first day of the week that Jesus rose triumphantly from the grave. It was the day that Jesus broke open the tomb and set us free from the bondage of sin and death!

Historically, holidays were times not only for rest but for remembrance—remembering what the other six days (or six months) of work are all about. They were times for regaining one's perspective, for reprioritizing, for having a sense of spiritual renewal.

Today's nonstop recreational vacations miss the point. Fast-paced as they are, they cannot fairly be said to be a change of pace from the working world. Most people are so exhausted after a vacation that they need a vacation just to rest up from all the activity!

That's why vacations ought really to be *holidays*—"holy" days, as it were. Times of quiet relaxation and reflection. Times of remembering what life is all about before it completely passes us by unnoticed. And times when we can get back to God, perhaps by getting closer to nature so that we can feel

God through his creation. More than just being fun, times of outdoor *recreation* should be times of inner *re-creation*.

Sadly, too few people know God well enough to recognize him while they are enjoying the beauty of his creation. But at least a holiday gives them the *opportunity* to see God. The solitude and quiet is ideally suited for reflection and personal introspection.

If Jesus were on the earth today, I suspect that he would love a holiday in the Cotswolds. Time after time, when the press of the crowds and the stress of opposition surrounded him, Jesus would go off alone—off to a quiet place—to seek solitude and share communion with the Father. Sometimes he took his disciples with him: "Because so many people were coming and going that they did not even have a chance to eat, he said to them, 'Come with me by yourselves to a quiet place and get some rest.' So they went away by themselves in a boat to a solitary place."

Wherever we are, God is always close. But as Jesus himself demonstrated, there is something about quiet times and quiet places that helps *us* to get closer to *God*. That special solitude provides a time of rest and renewal from a secular world that is busily ignoring God. It is a time of remembering *who* we are and *why* we are.

In the Cotswolds, I experience daily the words of that great hymn written by I. B. Sergei:

> My God and I go through the fields together.
> We walk and talk, as good friends should and do.
> We clasp our hands, our voices ring with laughter.
> My God and I walk through the meadow's hue.
>
> He tells me of the years that went before me,
> When heavenly plans were made for me to be.

When all was but a dream of dim conception,
To come to life, earth's verdant glory see.

For those who walk hand in hand with Jesus, *every* day is a holiday—a *holy* day before God. Some of us are specially blessed to have a life more conducive to the peace and quiet of holy days before God. But as someone who finds himself thrust back each year into the harsh reality of big-city madness, I know that the greater challenge is to find God in the midst of a metropolis. To see his hand in the inner city and among the urban sprawl; to find time for him in an already-overbooked schedule; to find a quiet place amid a constant bedlam of noise.

If we don't take the time to remember, we're in danger of forgetting his blessings. Therefore, take a few moments every day, if possible, or perhaps plan ahead to spend an afternoon walking in prayer with him. Whenever you feel your hand slipping from his, take some extra time to remember all that he has meant to you. And why not write down some of his special blessings throughout the year?

In whatever way best seems to help you remember, give yourself a treat, and book a holiday with God. Your life will be so much richer if you do!

Chapter Twenty

"Grow in the grace
and knowledge of
our Lord and Savior
Jesus Christ."

2 Peter 3:18

Exercise

There are any number of reasons for my daily walks in the Cotswolds. The beauty, the relaxation, the solitude—they all call out to me, "Come!" And so each day I head up into the hills. But this year my daily walks became part of a regimen of keeping fit, and may have turned out to be a lifesaver.

Walking in the Cotswolds is hard work if you're not used to it, and I haven't always been in the best of shape. In the past there has been a lot of huffing and puffing, moaning and groaning.

But this year was different. I knew something had to give. There had been too many books written under the pressure of deadlines. Too much chocolate and cheese nibbled through the night. There was too much sitting and not enough moving about. And far too much weight! It was time to do something about my body—to eat right and to get proper exercise.

Although I had always taken my walks, it was time now for some serious trekking: longer hikes, higher hills. Each day I headed out with renewed determination. Just one more field, one more fence; another ten minutes, another half-hour. I walked and walked until I nearly dropped.

Day after day, week after week, I went through my grueling paces. To my surprise, the dividends were quick in coming, and the weight fell off in sheets. By the end of the second month I had lost (in British terms) two stones. That's 28 hard-earned pounds, not to mention three inches in the waist. Lean and mean, I am now only half the man I used to be!

More amazing than the weight loss has been the increase in stamina. Sloping hills that I once considered mountains are now molehills. Steep climbs are taken in stride.

The apostle Paul must have climbed a few hills in his own day, or perhaps run a race or two. He had a fondness for using sports and exercise as illustrations of godly principles. When discussing the spiritual race we each must run, Paul points out the correlation between the hard work of exercise and winning the prize: "Everyone who competes in the games goes into strict training. They do it to get a crown that will not last; but we do it to get a crown that will last forever."

His contrast between the "crown that will not last" and the "crown that will last forever" fits nicely with his later distinction between two types of exercise. When he wrote to the young evangelist Timothy, the aging apostle reminded him that exercise of the body has only limited utility. "For physical training is of some value," said Paul, "but godliness has value for all things, holding promise for both the present life and the life to come."

In view of life's fleeting moment, the value to be found in spiritual exercise becomes more and more important. If *physical* exercise is good for losing weight and keeping fit, then *spiritual* exercise is good for "all things"! Did you catch the word Paul used as the equivalent of "spiritual exercise"? He used the word *godliness*—indicating that godliness is a matter of *exercise*! To put it plainly, godliness—being exercise—is *hard work*. It involves *pain* to get the gain.

From his own experience of learning about life through diligence and study, Solomon describes in some detail what spiritual exercise is all about: "If you *call out* for insight and *cry aloud* for understanding," says Solomon "then you will understand the fear of the Lord and find the knowledge of God." Make no mistake about it, he says emphatically—despite all the gain, inevitably there will be pain!

The good news is that, with God's strength, no "hill" is too high, no "journey" too long. As the prophet Habakkuk put it, "The Sovereign Lord is my strength; he makes my feet like the feet of a deer, he enables me to go on the heights."

The hilly Cotswolds are like tiny bumps in the ground compared with the spiritual heights to which I can climb with God as my strength. Listen as Isaiah describes those heights: "He gives strength to the weary and increases the power of the weak. Even youths grow tired and weary, and young men stumble and fall; but those who hope in the Lord will renew their strength. They will soar on wings like eagles; they will run and not grow weary, they will walk and not be faint."

What a thought! "They will run and not grow weary, they will walk and not be faint." And what a promise: *They will soar on wings like eagles!*

It's kind of nice how it all works out. If through physical exercise I am now *half* the man I used to be, through spiritual exercise I can be *twice* the man I used to be.

I wonder if that's how Moses felt when he sensed God's strength after crossing the Red Sea. "The Lord is my strength and my song," said Moses jubilantly; "he has become my salvation." Never are we stronger than when we are strong in the Lord!

I think what I've appreciated most from regular exercise is the *staying power* it provides. How much more then does *spiritual stamina* result from spiritual exercise! As the psalmist put it, "Blessed are those whose strength is in you, who have set their hearts on pilgrimage....They go *from strength to strength.*"

Joshua is a good example of a man who had spiritual stamina. When he was 85 years old he was still going strong, because God had given him the strength to carry out the work he had been given to do. "Now then," said Joshua, "just as the Lord promised, he has kept me alive for forty-five years....So here I am today, eighty-five years old! I am still as strong today as the day Moses sent me out; I'm just as vigorous to go out to battle now as I was then." Eighty-five and still out there fighting battles!

What battles are you facing? Wouldn't you like to know that God is your strength and staying power no matter what happens? "Sure," you say, "but what is the secret to having that kind of strength?"

That's the question Delilah kept asking the strongman, Samson, on behalf of the Philistines. She was so insistent that he eventually told her his secret: "No razor has ever been used on my head," he said, "because I have been a Nazarite set apart to God since birth. If my head were shaved, my strength would leave me, and I would become as weak as any other man."

When Delilah betrayed Samson and cut his hair, his strength left him. It was not the hair itself that counted, of course, but what it *symbolized*: his vow of commitment before God. *With* God's strength, Samson was twice the man he ever could have been otherwise. *Without* God's strength, he was but half the man he had been.

King David also knew what it meant to be strong in the Lord. When the Lord delivered David from the hands of his enemies and from Saul, David could hardly contain his excitement: "With your help I can advance against a troop; with my God I can scale a wall....It is God who arms me with strength and makes my way perfect."

Are there walls in your life that seem impossible to climb over? Maybe it's godly exercise that you need. Who knows what heights you might scale when you come to trust in the strength of the Lord? "With God, all things are possible." Paul believed it so much that he jubilantly proclaimed, "I can do everything through him who gives me strength!"

Knowing we have that kind of strength makes it possible to face whatever challenge or temptation might be just over the next horizon. Keeping spiritually fit prepares us for the future. I think here of the "wife of noble character" of Proverbs 31, of whom it was said, "She is clothed with strength and dignity; she can laugh at the days to come."

Wouldn't you love to have the kind of strength that enables you to "laugh at the days to come"? To know that, no matter what struggle or pain might be in store, you can be strong enough in the Lord to take on the future with confidence?

Of course, the idea of getting fit always *sounds* great. Why else do all the exercise bikes, rowing machines, and health spa memberships sell so well? But it's the *follow-through* that seems lacking. Ever notice how many exercise bikes and rowing machines gather dust in the corner of family rooms and basements, or how those first well-intentioned trips to the health spa have ultimately led to that cushy couch in front of the television?

The truth is that if we are ever going to grow stronger in the Lord, *we are going to have to work at it.* Every spiritual fiber within us will have to be stretched—even to the point of pain. The pain may come in the time we must carve out of already-busy schedules to do daily Bible reading; or it may come in the challenge of something which seriously needs changing in our lives.

Why are we willing to spend any number of years preparing for a profession or career, yet have little or no time for studying God's Word? Do we really expect to grow spiritually when we aren't willing to expend the necessary effort? And how can we enthusiastically spend an hour or two each day walking, jogging, or doing Jazzercise, yet complain when we have to spend an hour or two each week exercising our souls in worship to God? Just think what kind of shape our bodies would be in if the priorities were reversed!

It's time we took a good long look at ourselves. What do we see? Do we have healthy bodies, tanned and toned, but sagging souls which haven't had a proper spiritual workout for years? Have we learned the value of diet and exercise for the *package*—which one day will be discarded as so much extra baggage—but ignored the eternal destiny of the *person*?

Stretching our souls simply has to become our top priority. Not tomorrow, but *today!*

Chapter Twenty-one

"You are worth
more than
many sparrows."

MATTHEW 10:31

Sheep Droppings

A nuisance. Messy. To be avoided at all cost! On my walks I am never far from being reminded about why I always wear my "Wellie" boots, whether winter or summer, rainy season or drought. It's not just because of the winter mud, which can get so thick that it sucks a boot right off my foot, or because of the tall summer thistles, which reach out to sting any unprotected flesh. The reason for the boots is to cope with the sheep droppings and manure left behind by the local cows and horses.

You probably haven't given much thought to sheep droppings, have you? As it happens, on my walks I often find myself in a ponderous mood, oblivious. My head bowed in concentration, what passes before my eyes—whether or not I am always conscious of it—are thousands of these animal droppings.

Manure is many things to many people. For veterinarians, it's a clinical specimen; for farmers and gardeners, fertilizer. Unfortunately, for most people these days, manure is just another four-letter vulgarity, seemingly obligatory for comedians and box office success.

For the creative roofer who recently came to my rescue after the latest winter storm, it became the paint with which he toned down some stark grouting around newly-replaced stone slates. Phil strode confidently into the field next to the cottage, returned with a bucket of cow manure, and, by adding a bit of water, quickly had himself some homemade paint—in exactly the right color!

Only here in England would I have discovered that there apparently are such things as connoisseurs of animal manure. Alongside local roads I see scrawled signs advertising cow manure, pig manure, and horse manure—all at 65p or so a bag—each type obviously a crucial option for the discriminating manure buyer.

When I look about me and see sheep droppings all over the hillsides, there is something amazing about this most mundane expression of created matter. It's not nearly as contemptuous or loathsome as people might think. Manure is about as natural as anything can be. It is *of nature*. It is part of the natural order, with heavy emphasis on *order*. When the sheep leave their droppings, the droppings fertilize the ground, which gives life to the grass, which the sheep eat, which in turn gives them life-sustaining nourishment—and then the cycle begins all over again. It's a mini eco-system!

And that is where it occurs to me that we've missed the boat when we use another seemingly-innocuous substitute for "sheep droppings." It's that word *waste*. Human waste; animal waste. What could be more inappropriate than describing so valuable a contributor to the cycle of nature as nothing but waste, as if it had no place, no function, no purpose? We *waste* opportunities. We *waste* efforts. Sadly, we often even *waste* lives. But manure is rarely ever truly wasted. If it seems ugly, it is transformed. If it decomposes, it brings renewed life.

We all know what people are feeling when they say, in effect, "I feel like sheep droppings." Sometimes I feel that way too. But maybe that's the very time when I need to take another walk in the fields, just to remind myself. What a great God I must have who transforms sheep droppings into a source of renewal and life! For if even sheep droppings can serve a noble purpose, what reason could I ever have to think that God won't use my life for something worthwhile?

Behind the scenes, lurking somewhere deep down in all of us, is the haunting question of destiny: Do we really have anything special to contribute, or are we just rather ordinary? Ironically, how we answer that question may just answer that question! How we feel about our own usefulness to God can be a self-fulfilling prophecy.

I think of that "one-talent" servant in the parable of the talents. In the story, the master went on a journey and entrusted his property to his servants. To one he gave five talents of money, to another two talents, and to another one talent. The five-talent servant invested the five talents and got five more in interest. The two-talent servant followed suit, and gained an additional two talents. But the insecure one-talent servant hid his talent in a hole, drawing a sharp reprimand upon the master's return. Today we might cite the one-talent servant as an example of "using it or losing it."

God has blessed each of us with gifts of his own choosing. With these gifts, we've all got an important role to play. Ours will not always be the starring role, or even the role we might prefer. But there are people in your life and mine that only we can nurture in the way God has specially gifted us. Consequently, God needs us wherever we are, doing what we do best.

Remember Israel's battle with the Amalekites in which Moses held aloft the staff of God? As long as he held it high, Israel would surge forward in victory. When he dropped his hands, Israel would begin to lose. In the battle, there were two unlikely heroes, Aaron and Hur, who saved the day. "When

Moses' hands grew tired, they took a stone and put it under him and he sat on it. Aaron and Hur held his hands up—one on one side, one on the other—so that his hands remained steady till sunset." With that simple gesture the victory went to Israel.

Who was more useful on that day? The soldiers and generals in the field with all their bravery and courage? Moses with the staff of God in his hands representing the weighty responsibility of leading the nation? Or two men whose only job was to prop up Moses' hands? The truth is that each man played an important role—none any more or less important than any other. Sometimes the most useful thing we can ever do is to hold up the hands of those who lead us spiritually. Theirs is an awesome responsibility!

Our own bodies are also lessons about usefulness. "If the whole body were an eye, where would the sense of hearing be? If the whole body were an ear, where would the sense of smell be? But in fact God has arranged the parts in the body, every one of them, just as he wanted them to be. If they were all one part, where would the body be?" Just as in our own bodies, in which each part is vital, in Christ's body, the church, no member of the body is left without an important role to play.

The problem is that most of us have difficulty appreciating just how unique and special a gift we have been given. Often that's because the world's values are so upside-down. In Hollywood, only mega-stars get Oscars. (You can bet that the night watchman and the receptionist will never even get nominated!) But in the eyes of God, "those parts of the body that seem to be weaker are indispensable, and the parts that we think are less honorable we treat with special honor." In heaven, the first shall be last and the last shall be first!

Had any feelings lately about being useless? Do you look at others in the church who seem to contribute in really important ways while you're doing well just to greet the visitors?

Ever wish you had the ability to preach like the evangelist or had a burning desire to be a missionary in some foreign country, when you feel more comfortable helping your neighbors and visiting the sick? What a pity it would be to think that your life was a waste. God is already using you!

We don't have to be in a foreign country to be missionaries. God has given each one of us a mission, whether it be to our neighbors, the sick, or even to those who join us in worship as visitors. In God's eyes, no task we do is too great, nor any task too small. Along with Esther, who courageously approached the king on behalf of her people and thereby delivered them from certain death, who knows but that you have been brought into the kingdom "for such a time as this"?

Whenever I start to think that I'm useless, or that my life is a total waste, I remember that "the whole duty of man" is to "fear God and keep his commandments." If I did nothing more than worship and serve the Creator, my life would be worthwhile.

But when even that thought is not enough to dispel feelings of uselessness, I know that it's time to walk up into the hills and take another look at what lies at my feet. Praise God for sheep droppings! They reassure me that I have a Maker who doesn't want any part of his creation to go to waste! Especially me.

Chapter Twenty-two

"Do this in
remembrance
of me."

LUKE 22:19

The Cemetery

Not often, but on rare occasions, I pause for a moment at the gate leading to the village cemetery. It's always quiet and peaceful there, as one might expect. And along with "quiet" and "peaceful," I'm sure that "lovely" is also the right word, although it seems an odd term for a place so closely associated with the sadness of death.

Situated across the lane from the old churchyard, which itself is covered with gravestones from a more ancient era, the newer cemetery is entered through a wooden gate in the stone wall which surrounds it. Beyond the gate, a pebble path leads to a tall spreading evergreen, which commands attention like a striking centerpiece in a neatly-arranged funeral bouquet.

Behind the evergreen, and on either side, are the 50 or so graves which lie neatly in rows of six. Most of the graves are marked by simple upright stones at the head of each plot. While some of the graves are remembered with bunches of freshly-cut flowers, one grave is permanently covered with heather, and another has its own elegant blanket of deep purple petunias which embraces the entire ground.

Of course, one expects a cemetery to be a place of serenity. Appropriately, the weathered brass plaque on a solitary wooden bench reads: "Rest and be grateful."

Sometimes when I lean on the gate and survey the loveliness of the cemetery, I wonder what it would be like to see my own grave there. For most of my life I couldn't have cared less what happened to my earthly remains once I'm gone. *How* I might be buried or *where* never seemed to matter. But lately I've spread the word: "Bury me in Buckland. Perhaps back over there in the shade of that tree."

It shouldn't really make any difference one way or the other what might become my "final resting place." It will not be my final resting place in any event. Heaven will be my home— and it will be the loveliest resting place of all.

Nevertheless, with each year and with each loved one that passes, I am beginning to understand more clearly the importance of memorials. They help us remember how a person's life affected us, or perhaps made a lasting impression—maybe even changed us forever. Somewhere down there deep within us we have a compelling need to remember.

That is what intrigues me about the commitment I have made as a Christian. At the point when I made that commitment, I celebrated it through the ceremony of baptism—a symbolic memorial of Christ's own death, burial, and resurrection. As I entered the watery grave, I died to a world of sin and was buried like my own Lord. Through my surrender to him, I participated in his death and was washed spiritually clean by the power of his sacrificial blood. It was a magnificent moment!

But if I had never come out from under the water, what good would it have done me? I would have drowned, and my symbolic death literally would have become my grave. Instead, I was joyously raised in the likeness of Jesus' own resurrection.

Coming out of the water completed the picture: death, burial, *and* resurrection. What a fitting memorial for the Christian!

And what an appropriate message for the believer. Just as with the village cemetery, so too this special memorial provides a link with the past, a serenity for the present, and a certainty about the future. For in that unlikely act of humility—getting myself dunked in a pool of water in front of family and friends—I identified in faith with the Creator God who existed before the world began, with the Savior of the world in whose joyous presence I daily live, and with the God-acting-within-me Holy Spirit, who reassuringly seals the promise of an eternal life to come.

Can you think of anything more amazing than Christ inviting us to share with him in his death, burial, and resurrection? Are we worthy of such divine comparison? And yet in God's eyes, even baptism is not blessing enough. How much more amazing that he should care enough to provide us with an *ongoing* remembrance.

Perhaps you have experienced the death of someone especially close. If so, you'll know all too well that the funeral and the burial never seem to fully assuage our sense of loss, or to provide that crucial connection which we all so desperately want with those who have gone on before. That's why we periodically visit the graves. That's why so many loved ones regularly leave flowers in memory of the dead, who will neither see the flowers nor smell their fragrance.

So it is that in a similar way our need for an ongoing connection with Christ is met as we faithfully take the elements of communion with other believers. Like baptism, our participation in "the Lord's supper" is an altogether appropriate memorial, having been chosen by Christ himself in the upper room. "And he took bread, gave thanks and broke it, and gave it to them, saying, 'This is my body given for you; do this in remembrance of me.' In the same way, after the supper he took the cup, saying, 'This cup is the new covenant in my blood, which is poured out for you.'"

But there is more to this memorial than remembrance of things past. Through the bread and the wine, I catch a glimpse of the future. For Scripture tells us that whenever we eat the bread and drink the cup, we proclaim the Lord's death until he comes. Imagine it! What a powerful proclamation!

Without that hope—that Jesus Christ will come again and take us to himself in the heavenly realm—no cemetery could be described as lovely. Without the hope of life after death, cemeteries would be but sad monuments to hopelessness. But in Christ, there *is* hope. And eternal beauty. And loveliness forever.

So bury me in Buckland, but let your tears be few. It's not the shade of the tree in which I'll rest content, but in the shadow of his sheltering wings, where there will be no remembrance of things past—only sublime loveliness forever and ever.

Yet if we really believe this about our eternal destiny, then why don't we have more of a heart for heaven? Why don't we live each day more and more in anticipation of our eternal home? Someone once said, "Everybody wants to go to heaven, but nobody wants to die." That's our quandary, isn't it? Are we *heaven*-bound, or *earth*-bound? How many of us are ready to say along with Paul, "To live is Christ and to die is gain"?

How often during the day do we stop to remember what our life is really all about? At what moments in our life do we reflect upon the nearness of eternity? Solomon said that God has "set eternity in the hearts of men." In the busy bustle of each day, do *you* have a sense of eternity in *your* heart?

I'm not talking here about "living each day of your life as if it were the last." For all its commendable intent, not one of us could function if that were actually our daily thought. The world would come to a screeching halt. But having eternity in our hearts would make a world of difference in how we live each day.

If only the psalmist's prayer could be our own: "Teach us to number our days aright, that we may gain a heart of wisdom." Being reminded of the brevity of life focuses our attention on the bigger picture. When we remember that this life is but the doorway to eternal life, then pain is more easily endured; so too disappointment and loss—even the loss of those who have gone before us into eternity!

Getting the right perspective is important for fully appreciating the purpose of our existence, and in turn for setting proper priorities. Would we not be more caring toward others, and more likely to deal with the sin in our lives? Would we not spend more time in prayer and praise? How could we even think of putting careers ahead of relationships, or fail to see opportunities for sharing with others the good news of Christ!

Having eternity in our hearts is a continuous, *moment-by-moment* reminder of what our one-time baptism and our ongoing participation in the Lord's Supper is meant to picture: the new life that we have because of the death of him who triumphed over the grave. The new life that no cemetery, no matter how lovely, can ever contain. New life fit for eternity, and new life fit for the here and the now of today. This *very* day.

And *every* day, lest we too soon forget!

In loving memory of Mollie Worgan
in whose life was hope, and beauty, and loveliness.
1936-1991

Chapter Twenty-three

"Set your
hearts on
things above."

COLOSSIANS 3:1

The Hunt

I t's one of those rare, magical sights. Look! Over there. Quick! In early spring, when cold winds sweep across the hills, and mornings still bring a crispness to the air, I occasionally see a lone, sleek fox running with proud elegance across the hillside. I tell you, there's nothing like that sight. Nearby, what's exciting for me must be chilling for the rabbits scurrying into their burrowed hedgerow hideaways. The sheep, too, keep a wary eye on the fox's every movement.

Sometimes I can just catch a glimpse of some prized trophy being carried away in the fox's mouth. There will be a fine dinner at his table tonight.

The fox undoubtedly enjoys his reputation for being cunning. He always seems to get his prey. But do you suppose he is aware of nature's rhythm in which the *hunters* inevitably become the *hunted*? Or does the fox take security in knowing that the cycle of nature in an increasingly civilized world is less threatening than it once was for animals in the wild? Natural predators who might fancy the fox for their own dinner are less likely to have access to his habitat.

It could be a costly mistake, however, if the fox misjudged the safety of his environment. Any day now, he may discover that he has some unexpected adversaries—an unlikely alliance of man, horse, and hound.

The time-honored English hunt is a tradition that most foxes would rather miss—unless they are terribly sporting, and derive some sinister pleasure out of leading hound, horse, and man on a merry chase o'er hill and dale until the partygoers have had their fill of bumps, bruises, and spills. A smart fox knows that the odds of his actually being caught are less than the odds of the bungling Keystone cops catching the robbers they chase!

I must admit that I get goosebumps every time I hear the distant sound of the hunter's horn calling the hounds to the fore. My adrenaline begins to flow as the barking hounds come nearer and nearer.

I'll never forget standing in my back garden one day, peering in anticipation of seeing the hounds, when all of a sudden here they were, dashing over, under, and sometimes through my fence! There was no end to them, frantically chasing around in circles in a desperate attempt to follow the scent of the fox.

My mind raced at the thought that horses and riders would soon be following them across my back garden. Fortunately, they headed up the equestrian trail to the side of the cottage and then turned back along the paved village lane. The loud clippity-clop of the horses' shoes constituted the percussion section of a beautifully orchestrated concert of color and movement. The horses themselves were dashing, with every sinew strained for the pursuit. The riders were decked out in formal hunting jackets of dark blue and royal red, set off nicely with traditional riding hats and shiny black boots resting in silver stirrups. Philip Smith, my neighbor up the lane, was wearing his formal top hat, as if he were on his way to the House of Lords.

It's the very picture you probably have of rural England! But there is always something wonderfully comical about the whole adventure: The fox is chasing his freedom; the hounds are chasing the fox; the horses and riders are chasing the hounds; and—adding delightful confusion to the entire affair—scores of excited onlookers in cars and on bicycles are chasing the hunt!

As leisure activities go, one man's football is another's English hunt. If you happen to think hunting is a cruel sport, it is nevertheless a *sport*. When all is said and done, it is a mostly-traditional form of activity lacking any truly significant substance.

Unlike the fox himself, who, when he hunts, hunts in dead earnest for his dinner, the hunters will finish the day at the local pub, quaffing an ale or two and recounting the day's excitement. It hardly matters whether the supposed object of their hunt—the fox—has been taken. In truth, of course, we know that the real object of the hunt was never the fox in the first place. The *excitement itself* was the object of the hunt!

I confess there are times when I wonder what I myself am chasing. Is life for me a serious pursuit, or is it a comical charade in which I spend my time striving after any number of rather meaningless objects? When I am in the fast lane of a frenetic culture far from the peaceful English countryside, Solomon's advice hits home with particular force: "Better one handful with tranquillity than two handfuls with toil and chasing after the wind."

I like to think that I'm not chasing after materialism, but who am I kidding? Like many of us, I don't particularly want a lot of money; I just want the good life that money can buy! And in that goal I get caught up in the misguided confusion of chasing others, who themselves are chasing society's style-setters, who in turn set the pace in deciding what we all ought to be chasing.

Keeping up with the Joneses is not just about money or materialism; it's all about the frantic lifestyle of our time: the endless pursuit of greater and greater achievement, and the lust for power or recognition. If I'm honest with myself, much of what I chase after is immediate physical gratification rather than long-term spiritual fulfillment—a meaningless life exercise having little to do with anything soul-enriching or eternal.

All that would be bad enough, but when I step back and think about it, I realize that there is a great irony at work here. Foxes, who chase (and viciously kill) rabbits and lambs, are themselves chased by other predators. The *hunters* always become the *hunted*. In our desperate search for earthly fulfillment, humans are hunted down by *the very things they chase after*! Accumulation brings fear of loss; achievement begs even more herculean effort; and recognition robs me of privacy. When that happens, *who* is chasing *whom*?

In his Sermon on the Mount, Jesus warned us about how our "chasings" can end up being robbed of everything we chase after. "Do not store up for yourselves treasures on earth," he said, "where moth and rust destroy, and where thieves break in and steal." If we chase about accumulating wealth, says Jesus, we only invite others to start chasing us in turn so that they can steal it away from us. Through our very efforts to accumulate, *we* become the hunted!

Jesus even uses the picture of "chasing" to describe how those he classes as pagans get their priorities all wrong. "Do not worry, saying, 'What shall we eat?' or 'What shall we drink?' or 'What shall we wear?' For the pagans run after all these things, and your heavenly Father knows that you need them."

Strictly speaking, food, clothing, and shelter do not count as the accumulation of wealth. They are "necessities." Yet Jesus says that "chasing after" even those things is the hunt of pagans, not the hunt of God's people! Why? Because we forget that God provides what we need, and that we only end up being consumed by the effort and energy we expend in trying to make sure that we have even the basics.

Isn't it strange? In chasing after all the style and excitement this world has to offer, we end up being victimized by our own pursuits! It's as if the rabbit turned on the fox, or the fox turned on the horses and their riders!

There is a way out of this vicious circle. It comes by *seeking*, not by chasing. In his Sermon on the Mount, Jesus urged us to "seek first his kingdom and his righteousness, and all these things will be given to you as well." If we spend our time seeking God, we will never be disappointed. We will never be empty, or searching, or discontent. There will be no reason to chase after *illusive* happiness, for in Christ, *true* happiness is within our grasp!

Chapter Twenty-four

"My comfort in my
suffering is this:
Your promise
renews my life."

PSALM 119:50

Five Black Cows

A year or so ago, I thought my daily walks might come to an end. It was foolish what I had done. Using my right leg, I had stepped down hard on a long piece of wood that I was holding at an angle in my left hand. The idea was to break the piece of wood in two. When the wood finally gave way to the pressure, so did my right knee. That's when the panic set in.

I soon found that I could barely walk, and only with the greatest effort could I descend the stairs. For two days I gave the knee a rest, trying not to walk on it at all. Then I thought it might be best to give the knee a cautious workout.

With my trusty walking stick in hand, I dragged myself out of the cottage and onto the narrow equestrian trail leading to the next village. Limping like an old man, I plodded my way ever so slowly to an open pasture which led up the hill. Walking uphill seemed a little less painful, but I was clearly in trouble. I decided it was time to see the doctor.

Onward I struggled, step after careful step, until I reached a path leading back toward the village. The path wound its way from one field to another, where I climbed carefully over the fence separating the two. English walking paths have any number of ingeniously constructed stiles, and I was fortunate on this occasion to find one that could well have merited a designation for the disabled.

Once safely over the fence, I looked up to see five very familiar faces—five very familiar *bovine* faces, to be precise. I can't tell you how many times my daily walks had taken me past these same five black cows. Never before had they paid me the slightest bit of attention. Whenever I would pass by, it was always munching as usual.

But this day was strangely different. This day all munching stopped as they turned to curiously note my bent frame and tentative gait. Then, to my great amazement, they slowly began following me, in single file—something they had never done before—as if to say, "Let's walk with the old guy for a while."

I soon became lost in thought. Then, all of a sudden, I heard the sound of cows running toward me. I turned around to see the five black cows rapidly bearing down on me, this time as if to say, "Enough of this limping stuff, let's run for a while!" Seeing me stand my ground in front of them, they skidded to a halt and began playfully butting heads with each other.

As I turned back around and started to walk away, I realized that I could walk again! Praise God, I was healed! First one step and then another. Even downhill. There was some residual pain, but I could tell that the knee was working properly again. "Let this story get out," I chuckled to myself, "and my little village with its five sacred cows will become another Lourdes."

On my way back to the cottage, I wondered what I would have thought if I had prayed for a healing just as I was climbing over the fence into the field with the five black cows.

Would I not have attributed my healing to a divine miracle? And why not? I was thankful to God in any event.

I have no doubt that God can, and does, bring healing. As James assures us in his epistle, fervent prayer may well be the avenue through which such a miracle of healing comes. But Jesus did not attempt to heal every suffering person during his ministry. God's greater concern is about my spiritual health, and perhaps about how I might *respond* to having a broken body.

Rather than being the cause of my healing out there in the field, I suspect that God was much more like the five black cows. They weren't there to heal me that day, but they seemed to sense something different about me and may well have decided to "walk with the old guy for a while."

For me, that is all I need to know about the Great Physician. Whether he heals me or not, I'll still give him all the praise. He knows better than I do what's best for me. It's enough simply to know that there is always Someone who is willing to walk with me, no matter how badly my life is limping along.

I join with the apostle Paul on this one: "Praise be to the God and Father of our Lord Jesus Christ, the Father of compassion and the God of all comfort, who comforts us in all our troubles!" It's not God's healing that I cherish so much as his "bedside manner."

David's psalm speaks of a father's compassion: "As a father has compassion on his children, so the Lord has compassion on those who fear him." But I love even more Isaiah's picture of God as a mother comforting her child: "Can a mother forget the baby at her breast and have no compassion on the child she has borne? Though *she* may forget, I will not forget you!"

We are God's children. Should we think that he doesn't know when we are hurting? Should we think that he doesn't care?

Isaiah could hardly contain himself at the thought of God's comfort: "Shout for joy, O heavens; rejoice, O earth; burst into song, O mountains! For the Lord comforts his people and will have compassion on his afflicted ones." If it gives us a warm feeling to imagine that a few stray cows might somehow care about the way we walk, how much greater a feeling we can have to know of a certainty that the Creator of the universe *truly* cares about how we feel!

But God's own comfort is one of those "pass-it-on" things. Earlier, I interrupted what Paul was saying about the God who comforts us in all of our troubles. There was a *so that* attached— "*so that* we can comfort those in any trouble with the comfort we ourselves have received from God."

As John Henry Jowett put it, "God does not comfort us to make us comfortable, but to make us comforters."

When I think of ordinary people comforting others, I think of Job's friends—Eliphaz, Bildad, and Zophar—who went "to sympathize with him and comfort him." Also the many friends who, when Lazarus died, came to Martha and Mary "to comfort them in the loss of their brother."

Surely these were simple gestures—nothing overwhelming or dramatic; nothing life-changing. Certainly not *circumstance*-changing. But they were expressions of love and the healing balm of comfort. "Comfort, comfort my people, says your God."

What do you say to the mourning couple who has just lost their child? Or to the friend whose spouse has just walked away from the marriage? What words can prove adequate for the person dying of cancer or other deadly disease? How do you possibly answer the grief-stricken "Why?" that follows the fatal auto crash?

In my earlier years, my attempts at comforting others were really attempts to somehow heal the situation. I thought I could capture just the right words or quote the perfect Scriptures to "make everything right." But now I realize the futility of trying to change the circumstances, as if a sufficient amount of carefully worded denial would mask the reality. The truth is, we can never "make everything right." Death, pain, sorrow, and the whole range of human suffering is a natural part of this world that won't just go away.

If there is insight and wisdom to be shared, or a word of Scripture that truly does speak to the situation at hand, then that can be a comfort. And joining together in prayer can itself be an act of compassion. But godly comfort need only join heart to heart in love. For comfort is not simply a matter of soothing or easing pain. The word *comfort* literally means to "make strong." When hearts join with other hearts, there is strength to withstand what one heart alone could not endure.

Nowadays, I mostly sit in silence. It's the quiet hug, the tender touch that brings comfort. That which is already known need not be spoken. Just our *being there* is what people need. To know that we care. To know that they don't have to bear the pain alone. To know that God has sent angels of mercy to attend them in their hour of distress.

We should not be surprised, therefore, when our own pain and suffering is accompanied by what seems to be an ominous silence from heaven. If we call out for answers and don't hear any, it doesn't mean that there *are* no answers. If we cry out for healing and healing never comes, it doesn't mean that God is insensitive. Heart to heart, he suffers with us in silence.

God's comfort does not always come in the form of healing. It doesn't always take away the pain or change the circum-stances. But just knowing that God is with us, whatever the circumstances, is enough for me.

I could be wrong about the five black cows. What cow would ever think, "Let's walk with the old guy for a while"? But what a comforting thought: God sensing everything that impacts our lives, and walking along with us—no matter how slight the limp, no matter how serious the suffering.

Chapter Twenty-five

"Those who cling
to worthless idols
forfeit the grace
that could
be theirs."

JONAH 2:8

Gargoyles

Sometimes when I walk up the village lane as I do each day, I look back at St. Michael's church and see the tower standing out in a kind of bas-relief against the sky. And what always catches my eye are the carved stone gargoyles anchoring the four corners of the tower just beneath the parapet. The gargoyles of St. Michael's are not famous, as are those at Notre Dame (romanticized by Victor Hugo and the etcher Meryon), but I still find them fascinating. Grotesque. Menacing. They look a frightful sight!

The original purpose of scary-looking gargoyles is somewhat obscure, yet in stark contrast to the church's realm of peace and salvation, they symbolized demon-haunted air and the world of the flesh and of the devil. Often the figures represented a particular evil or vice. A hog's face, for example, would represent gluttony.

In traditional Gothic architecture, gargoyles act as drainspouts, with rainwater gushing out of their open mouths. Two of the gargoyles on St. Michael's have large round metal pipes extending out of their mouths to improve the drainage.

But many gargoyles found on cathedrals and abbeys have no functional purpose whatever. They are simply chunks of carved stone placed strategically about, much like pagan idols. What fascinates me about the pagan-like features of gargoyles is that they are found on buildings in which Christian worship takes place. Here they are, warding off the evil spirits from what is supposed to be a house of God. Given the gloomy nature of Gothic architecture generally, and its association with the pagan Goths in particular, perhaps it shouldn't be surprising. But one does wonder!

My guess is that gargoyles are just another example of how those of us who are believers feel just a bit more comfortable when we can hedge our bets in terms of personal security. "In God we trust," or so we say, but when things are going well we still "knock on wood" just to make sure they stay that way. And when an imagined adversary comes toward us, we only half-jokingly hold up fingers in the form of a cross, as if to ward off its evil.

Look around on the dashboards of cars going by, and you'll still see plenty of St. Christophers, supposedly providing protection for the car's occupants. Superstition—be it reading the daily horoscope, going to your local psychic, or symbolically knocking on the wood of the cross—has never completely eluded even well-educated people.

Christian faith or no Christian faith, there are plenty of believers past and present who have been more than willing to "clasp hands with pagans," as Isaiah put it. Witness Jacob's wife, Rachel, who went so far as to steal her own father's household gods, despite being one of the honored progenitors of God's chosen nation, Israel. And at the very moment Moses was up on the mountain receiving the Ten Commandments, the Israelites were bowing down to a golden calf—only months after God had delivered them from Egyptian slavery through the miraculous parting of the Red Sea!

One of my favorite passages on idolatry comes again from Isaiah. It says it all. Speaking with acrid derision about a man who has made a wooden idol out of a felled tree, Isaiah describes this deliciously ironic scene:

> *Half of the wood he burns in the fire;*
> *over it he prepares his meal, he roasts his*
> *meat and eats his fill. He also warms*
> *himself and says, "Ah! I am warm; I see*
> *the fire." From the rest he makes a god,*
> *his idol; he bows down to it and*
> *worships. He prays to it and says, "Save*
> *me; you are my god."*

What a picture! I'd love to know if the churchmen responsible for placing the gargoyles on St. Michael's actually believed their grotesque figures could fend off "the evil eye," and, if so, whether it ever occurred to them that there could be little security in something which they themselves had made. Trusting such man-made images is nothing less than trusting in our own weakness!

The old television series asked the right question: "Who do you trust?" Who indeed! The psalmist could well have been referring to our fanciful gargoyles when he penned these words:

> *They have mouths, but cannot speak,*
> *eyes, but they cannot see;*
> *they have ears, but cannot hear,*
> *nor is there breath in their mouths.*
> *Those who make them will be like them,*
> *and so will all who trust in them.*

Whether it be in lifeless idols or whatever else it is that we look to for safety and security, we can never trust anything of our own making. Knowing that, the psalmist puts his trust in God whenever he has reason to fear:

> *He who dwells in the shelter of the*
> *Most High*
> *will rest in the shadow of the Almighty.*
> *I will say of the Lord, "He is my refuge and*
> *my fortress,*
> *my God, in whom I trust."*
> *You will not fear the terror of night,*
> *nor the arrow that flies by day,*
> *nor the pestilence that stalks in the darkness,*
> *nor the plague that destroys at midday.*

What then are the "gargoyles" in which we have put our trust for security? What idols do we depend on to save us in times of crisis? What do we depend upon to fend against hard times and adverse circumstances?

I suspect some of us would have to answer that it's the highly prized job security we've worked so hard to secure, or the bank accounts we build up. More likely these days, it's having that already-overloaded credit card to fall back on, or the insurance policy or pension fund.

Then again, our sense of security isn't always tied to materialism. It can be the wife looking for security in her husband, or the husband desperately needing a sense of support from his wife. Perhaps we rest our security in that college degree we've struggled to get, or some rung on the career ladder to which we've finally managed to climb. Or maybe it's surrounding ourselves with all the right friends and associates. Security comes in so many different packages!

The problem comes in sorting out genuine security from the counterfeits. Ancient Israel worshiped the God of heaven, but put her trust in fortified walls. The fortified walls crumbled before Israel's enemies! In a society which increasingly walls itself in from threats of street crime and escalating violence, in what are we placing our trust for daily survival? Can we truly say "In God we trust," or is our trust only in burglar alarms, security patrols, and handguns?

When Israel sought security in horses, chariots, and political alliances, the nation was in for a rude awakening. Military might failed them because they had their priorities wrong. The historical record says tersely that "they did not look to the Holy One of Israel, or seek help from the Lord."

As with Israel, so it is with families and individuals when priorities get mixed up. The man who spends every waking hour at the office trying to provide financial security for his family will have missed the greatest security he could ever give his wife and children: his involvement and spiritual concern in their lives. The woman who takes that extra job to make sure her children have everything she herself never had has miscalculated that which makes her children the most secure. It is not an abundance of *things* that will make them happiest, but knowing that someone who loves them is always near.

The problem with putting our trust in anything other than God is that it shrinks our view of God's infinite power. The specific details may vary, whether it's insurance policies, or handguns, or even relationships. But the real problem is that we worship a god too small.

Whatever is not of God is a gargoyle. Whatever is not of faith is only thinly masked paganism. It might as well be a wooden idol!

Never in our own time have paganism and Christian faith been so muddled together! Never have we as a society been more keen to hedge our spiritual bets, whether through the pluralistic acceptance of all religions, or through worshiping Mammon, the god of shopping malls, or even for literally worshiping ourselves!

Whatever faith-substitutes we might invest in, they all take us a giant step backward to ignorance, superstition, and spiritual darkness. Given their ability to deceive us into thinking that we are secure when we are not, our gargoyles are more grotesque and menacing than we might ever imagine! Worst of all, they drain away our faith, leaving us more alone and fearful than ever before.

Frightful as they are, somehow I prefer the gargoyles on St. Michael's. At least their crumbling features are a reminder of the futility of putting our trust in anything else but God. When we hedge our bets by what Isaiah referred to as "clasping hands" with the world around us, we hardly notice that what we end up trusting is our own fearful emptiness.

Why not join with the psalmist in joyfully proclaiming, "I will say of the Lord, 'He is my refuge and my fortress, my God, in whom I trust'"? With God on our side, there is no terror too great, no illness that can't be faced, no calamity that can't be overcome. Gargoyles—whatever ours may be—are empty and powerless. They cannot save. By sublime contrast, our God is *alive*, and in the shadow of *his* sheltering wings we can rest secure!

Chapter Twenty-six

"The spirit is
willing, but the
body is weak."

MATTHEW 26:41

The Greenhouse

Have you ever gone back to a favorite house where you once lived, only to be utterly disappointed to discover that something about it had changed drastically? This year for me was one of those memory-shaking times.

Refreshing, calming, and invigorating—my daily walks along the footpaths above Buckland have become a treasured ritual, a chance almost literally to inhale a peace and tranquility I find nowhere else. Each year when I return to my little cottage I can hardly wait to put on my green "Wellies," grab my rough-hewn walking stick, and head up into the hills. It's that glorious view I must see once again, always as if for the first time.

But this year was different. My first view down over the village held in store something I was not at all expecting. More than a surprise, it was a terrible shock! It was the sight of a new greenhouse, the size of two city blocks, blighting my treasured Cotswold village!

From the moment I first moved into my cottage, I had joined with others to protest my neighbor's plans to build the expanded greenhouse. But letters and phone calls to the planning council had proved futile. Permission had been granted and work already begun by the time I went away last autumn.

I suppose, then, that I should not have been so shocked. However, the view from above the village far exceeded my worst fears. The new structure, like a sea of glass awash in verdant fields of green, cast a graffiti-like reflection in the late afternoon sun. It was the unspoiled village itself which had once graced the horizon, but now the massive greenhouse, complete with smokestack and billowing puffs of steam, had stolen the show.

I wanted to scream in outrage! I even confess that a part of me wished there were some way to tear it down. It wasn't a loss in property values that concerned me, nor the advancing march of progress in a world already convulsing from too much change. At its core, the greenhouse was a gleaming vulgarity which profaned one of the last truly unspoiled pockets of beauty in the English countryside. It was so out of character that it was a desecration.

Am I alone in desperately wanting to hold onto some semblance of the tranquil and the traditional? To keep my perfect world? Is that too much for me to ask? Must something always come along to spoil the picture?

As I reflected on my anger and outrage, I began to wonder if that isn't the way God often views me. Does he look down on his glorious plan for my life and see how terribly I've profaned it?

Surely my sin blasphemes his call to purity. Surely it spoils the spiritual landscape. I don't know about you, but there is a part of my life that is unworthy of the rest of me which willingly bows in submission to his leading. Part of me which is ugly and unbefitting. It is so inconsistent with the rest of my character that it desecrates the whole.

I can join the apostle Paul in truthfully saying that I "delight in God's law" in my inner being. I *want* to do what's right. Deep down, at the bedrock of my faith, I am God's person. But like the apostle Paul, whose frank confession of spiritual struggle is a reminder of my own frustrating fallibility, I see "another law at work in the members of my body, waging war against the law of my mind and making me a prisoner of the law of sin at work within my members."

What I *want* to do in living my life before God is not always what I find myself actually doing. As Paul put it, "What I want to do I do not do, but what I hate I do." Like Paul, "I have the desire to do what is good, but I cannot carry it out."

I wish it were only moral frailty that I shared with the rest of humankind. But it gets worse. Sometimes I try to justify my moral inconsistency by reassuring myself that there's only one small part of me that rebels against God. "There's only one area of my life that I haven't given over to the Lord, so how bad can that be?" I ask myself by way of justification. Even if that were remotely true, of course, it would stand me in no better stead with the One who calls me to perfection in *every* area of my life.

Merely mention the word *perfection* and I get caught up in yet another self-deception. Knowing that God has promised his grace to those who love and trust him, I sometimes try another convenient escape route. "I can't possibly live without *some* inconsistency in my life," I tell myself. "After all, *I am human!* And that's what God's grace is all about. It makes up for human imperfection. So God doesn't expect me to be *totally* consistent between how I think and how I act." It's a seductive thought, isn't it?

Naturally, I'm not the first person tempted to trade cheaply on God's mercy. The streetwise apostle was way ahead of anyone who might see grace as an excuse for sin: "What shall we say, then? Shall we go on sinning so that grace may increase? By no means! We died to sin; how can we live in it any longer?"

Sin—even if not glaring in the eyes of the world—is always glaring to God. "Inconsistency" is hardly the word for lives lived even partially in rebellion to God. Why is it so hard for me to see my sin for what it really is?

When I think of the greenhouse, I am incensed and outraged. Oh, I can forgive my neighbor for doing what I might also be tempted to do if I were in his shoes. But it's hard for me to forget the result. Each daily walk is marred by its reflection.

Yet, would that I could be so incensed and outraged at my own sin—to want to tear it down, or blow it up! To write myself letters of protest! Am I to imagine that the sin which mars my daily walk with God is not reflected, like a mirror of glass, for all to observe? Do they not think that my life betrays what I profess to believe? With that thought, I deplore the new greenhouse all the more. Now it has become a daily reminder of my own imperfection.

Yet perhaps it can be a challenge rather than an affront. Perhaps it can motivate me to dismantle that part of me which is ugly and out of place. It won't be easy tearing down the glass house in which I've allowed myself to live for so long, but dismantle it I must. Pain by pain, if necessary.

Fortunately for all of us, there is a sense in which God himself does the dismantling. Jesus is at work in me, completing what he has already begun. As long as I live, he will continue to work with me so that who I am today is never the person I am yet to be. That which needs dismantling is being torn down. That which needs restoring is being built up.

In his wonderful chapter on love (1 Corinthians 13), Paul speaks of another kind of glass—the mirror we see through dimly. Though he intended a more theological application, nevertheless the same metaphor could apply to our own lives: "Now we see but a poor reflection as in a mirror; then we shall see face to face. Now I know in part; then I shall know fully, even as I am fully known." As we look into the mirror of our present lives, the person we see today is but a dim figure of the person that God has in mind for us to be.

Paul's words further suggest that our spiritual transition is a matter of growth, happening gradually as in the stages of one's life: "When I was a child, I talked like a child, I thought like a child, I reasoned like a child. When I became a man, I put childish ways behind me." The intriguing thing is that spiritual growth is not as natural as physical growth. Both body and soul need nourishment, but spiritual nourishment comes in the most surprising way—very much like what happens in my neighbor's greenhouse.

The greenhouse may be out of character on the outside, but what happens on the inside is truly a wonder. The most delicious tomatoes flourish there, without a particle of soil! Given proper nutrients and just the right environment, my neighbor's tomatoes grow more prolifically than they ever could under natural conditions.

The same is true of us. Left to our own nature, we end up absorbing the environment of the world in which we are naturally rooted. We grow, all right, but only in conformity with the values and character of the sinful world around us.

To become spiritual people, we need a different kind of nourishment. "Flesh gives birth to flesh, but the Spirit gives birth to spirit," said Jesus. And again, "The Spirit gives life; the flesh counts for nothing. The words I have spoken to you are spirit and they are life."

What could make tomato plants grow without soil is a mystery to most people. Even more of a mystery is the metamorphosis we undergo when we make the transition from *natural* to *spiritual*. What is the source of our new life? The same Spirit that raised Jesus from the grave! "If the Spirit of him who raised Jesus from the dead is living in you, he who raised Christ from the dead will also give life to your mortal bodies through his Spirit, who lives in you."

When God looks at me, he sees more than just the many ways in which I am noticeably out of character with his own goodness. What he sees is my spiritual destiny. As a result, he doesn't simply protest my sinfulness; he seeks ways to draw me closer to him. He isn't interested in destroying me in anger and outrage; rather, he looks for opportunities to nurture me into newness. Through his Spirit working in my innermost parts, God transforms my ugliness into beauty. He cultivates within me a transformed life that flourishes bountifully from the spiritual nutrients of his grace and love!

Today I took another walk, but this time alongside the greenhouse. For the first time, looking from ground level through the glass, I noticed the tomato plants themselves, row after neatly strung row. It gave me quite a different perspective than I had previously had from a distance. What I saw inside the greenhouse was a thing of beauty, and of life. There was a fascinating, almost miraculous process of growth taking place that would soon be providing enjoyment and nourishment all over England and beyond.

I don't know if I'll ever come to terms with the appearance of the greenhouse from my vantage point up in the hills while I'm walking. Probably not. But I must make a note to thank my neighbor for teaching me something very important about true beauty. With me, as with the greenhouse, the beauty lies within. And God knows that. Just when I get to thinking that I'm an unsightly greenhouse blighting his spiritual landscape, God takes me by the hand and shows me what he is growing on the inside.

No, I'll never reach the perfection I long for in my private world, especially not within myself. But neither am I destined to be an ugly greenhouse forever. If I let God accomplish the plans he has for my life, there will be no reason to dwell on the ugliness. With God's Spirit nourishing my life, there's going to be a profusion of spiritual growth that will burst right through the roof!

Chapter Twenty-seven

"Hear from heaven,
your dwelling place,
and when you hear,
forgive."

1 KINGS 8:30

RECONCILIATION

Sunsets

Transfixed, I stood watching a perfectly-round crimson sun hanging motionless above a distant line of trees, with bare wintry limbs reaching up as if to puncture the glowing roundness. I kept thinking how indescribable it was, how perfect beyond belief, wishing I could capture it on film, in words, in memory—anything. Finally I turned and walked to the corner of the plowed field, where I once again glanced back toward the west. In just those few short minutes, the sun's brilliance had already fled, and its sharp features had blurred into the darkened sky around it. What I had hoped to capture had gone.

Never are my walks more rewarding than when I am caught up in the beauty of a sunset. From neons to pastels, from brilliant to soft, sunsets bring the day to a close with a grace that surpasses anything else in all of nature. At what other moment is the world at such peace?

When I think of all the rich parables that can be drawn from my daily walks, I think that sunsets may speak to me most often. Sunsets are a daily declaration of the majesty of God. They speak of infinite beauty and of the power of him who created the incomparable realms of heaven and earth. They tell of God's greatness and, by comparison, my own smallness.

In sunsets, I see golden years of retirement and the gentle greying of older age. In their brightly focused light, I see life's meaning clearer and loved ones dearer. Sunsets also suggest the end of one's time on the earth—not with sadness or melancholy, but with mirrored reflection on a life lived in faith and with the vibrant expectation of a life yet to come.

However, the lesson I treasure most from sunsets comes from the tender imagery of the psalmist, who sees heaven reaching down to *kiss the earth*, and in that rapturous moment bring peace.

Heaven kissing earth? How does that happen? "Love and faithfulness meet together," says the psalmist; "righteousness and peace kiss each other. Faithfulness springs forth from the earth, and righteousness looks down from heaven." A more apt depiction of the trysting place between heaven and earth, between God and man, cannot be found.

What the psalmist describes is at the very heart of Christian teaching. For anyone who has ever been turned off at the thought of dry theology, it's nice to know that the heart, soul, and essence of Christian teaching can be captured in a sunset: Heaven has kissed the earth!

The story may actually begin in the slightly different wording of the text as found in the King James Version. "Mercy and *truth* are met together," says the classic translation. When God and man meet, it is nothing less than a meeting of mercy and truth—the *truth* being the unrighteousness of sinful man, and *mercy* being God's salvation of man from sin. What you and I corruptly bring forth during our time on the earth is embraced and covered over by what God mercifully brings down from heaven.

When modern translations speak of *love* and *faithfulness* meeting together in a divine embrace, it is not, as we might think, *our faithfulness* meeting *God's love*, because we are not faithful. You and I can never fully keep our promises to each other, much less to God. (Witness the many failed marriages and other failed social contracts.) Rather, it is God's own faithfulness, together with his merciful love, that brings us peace.

It is only because God's love and faithfulness have met together in a divine embrace that we are able to understand the "sunset" picture of *righteousness* and *peace* (heaven and earth, as it were) "kissing each other."

The peace of God is not the mere peace of tranquility, as in the "peacefulness of the Cotswolds." God's peace is harmony where there was disharmony; acceptance where there was rejection; rightness where there was wrongness. Because of God's own righteousness, whatever is wrong can be put right.

But what is the source of God's righteousness? The psalmist attributes it to God's love and faithfulness. God's *love* we see in the life and sacrificial death of Jesus Christ. "For God so loved the world," says the Bible's most memorized passage, "that he gave his one and only Son!"

God's *faithfulness* we see in the fulfillment of promise. The Messiah's coming had been prophesied for centuries, yet heaven and earth had remained separated by the mighty abyss of sin. In the birth of Jesus, God finally came near. In the birth of Jesus, both heaven and earth rejoiced! Little wonder that at the time of Jesus' birth the heavenly host proclaimed: "Glory to God in the highest, and on earth *peace* to men on whom his favor rests."

Jesus' birth—this "God come down to earth"—was all about peace between God and man, all about heaven kissing the earth!

The "sunset picture" of God's reconciling righteousness is found not only in the *birth* of Jesus, but even more so in the *death* of Jesus, for it was through his death on the cross that God "kissed" sinful man and brought us peace. Hung there on the cross—suspended between heaven and earth and silhouetted against the darkness of tragic gloom—Jesus died so that we might have our sins taken away. In the twilight of that awful day, it was not the setting *sun*, but his *Son* who set things right between God and man.

I confess that it's all a mystery—a wonderful, full-of-wonder mystery. Yet what a glorious picture Paul paints of our peace with God! In his letter to the Ephesians, Paul speaks of a barrier between Jews and Gentiles which has been broken down by Christ. With only the slightest shift in emphasis, he could well have been speaking of the barrier between a righteous God and sinful man: "For he himself [Christ] is our peace, who has made the two [God and man] one and has destroyed the barrier [sin], the dividing wall of hostility."

The inner peace which each of us seeks is found in our reconciliation with God—not that we *become* God, but that we are no longer alienated *from* God.

And who else could have brought about that reconciliation except "God made flesh," Jesus Christ? Who else could both destroy the "barrier" and build the "bridge"? "For God was pleased to have all his fullness dwell in him, and through him to reconcile to himself all things, whether things on earth or things in heaven, by making peace through his blood, shed on the cross."

Having God's peace does not mean that we will live trouble-free lives. What a great disillusionment it would be to think so! But along with Jesus' disciples we have his promise: "I have told you these things, so that in me you may have peace. In this world you will have trouble. But take heart! I have overcome the world."

Jesus reminds us that our peace is not boundless tranquility, as this world understands peace. It is an inner peace that can endure even the greatest of earthly troubles, knowing that all has been put right where it really matters: between ourselves and God. Because of God's love and faithfulness, even our greatest troubles can be transformed into triumph!

The sad thing about sunsets is that we miss so many of them. Busy lives and hectic schedules take us away from those precious moments each day when "heaven kisses the earth." What a greater shame that so many people miss the message of the cross: that heaven has kissed the earth in the person of Jesus.

At a time when society is frantically searching for inner peace, would that we could have the same assurance that the prophet Isaiah expressed. Led by the Spirit of God, Isaiah foresaw a time when heaven would no longer *need* to kiss the earth—a time when there will be no separation between heaven and earth as we know them, but peace forever in the presence of God.

"Your sun will never set again," Isaiah says with unbridled excitement, "and your moon will wane no more; the Lord will be your everlasting light, and your days of sorrow will end."

How I love sunsets, when heaven kisses the earth! But how I look forward to that eternal day when the sun will set no more.

> *Grace and love like mighty rivers*
> *Poured incessant from above,*
> *And heaven's peace and perfect justice*
> *Kissed a guilty world in love.*
> *—Robert Lowry*
> *(1826-1899)*

Chapter Twenty-eight

"Understanding is
a fountain of life to
those who have it."

PROVERBS 16:22

UNDERSTANDING

Cricket

The Beverly Hills of the Cotswolds! That's what I've come to call the immaculately groomed village of Stanton, two villages to the south of Buckland. Fortunately bereft of any tearooms or woolen shops with "Half-Price-Sale" signs in the windows, it has been spared the onslaught of tour buses and clamoring crowds of holiday makers.

Stanton has the look of a movie set. Take away the occasional car on the road and bring in some horse-drawn carriages, and the scene is perfectly set for an eighteenth- or nineteenth-century production. With only a little imagination, one can turn back the clock to another era, as happened recently in the filming of a Sherlock Holmes episode.

Indeed, one of England's great evangelists and hymnwriters, John Wesley, found Stanton to be a pleasant place of repose. One can almost see him arriving at the door of the village church, along with grey-suited gentlemen and ladies in their Sunday finest.

These days in Stanton, as throughout all of England, the hub of activity on the Lord's Day is more likely to be on the cricket pitch than in church pews. Though not terribly spiritual, still it must be said that a sporting game of cricket on Sundays in Stanton provides just that right finishing touch to a proper English village. With the participants decked out in their resplendent white uniforms against the background of a manicured green playing field, and with relaxed spectators spreading their picnic cloths around the outer boundaries, the quaint village scene is complete.

Occasionally, on a long Sunday afternoon circuit to Stanton, I pause on the perimeter of the cricket pitch to watch the action. However, I must confess that, for all its English trappings, my American instincts cause me to question using the word "action" in the same sentence with "cricket." No British game—not darts, not lawn bowling, not even snoozy snooker—could seem less exciting.

The closest American counterpart to cricket is baseball. But at least with baseball you have bench-clearing brawls, foot-long hot dogs, and the possibility that you might see a triple play or a no-hitter. With cricket, you often have to watch the same batter for hours; games can last for days; and everything is so prim and proper that they even take breaks for tea! Why would anyone want to spend a perfectly good afternoon playing—or watching—such a tedious and inscrutable game?

Naturally, cricket fans the world over would be offended that I should make disparaging remarks about a game which they easily understand and follow passionately. And I have to admit that if I understood the game better it probably wouldn't be boring at all. From what I can tell, cricket fans do at times get hysterically excited!

All of that makes me wonder if, for many people, the tables aren't turned when it comes to appreciating what it means to really know God. Are they mystified, for example, that people passionately believe in Someone they've never seen? Or that

Christians worship a God who has the power to create the universe, but then comes to earth in human form and allows himself to be killed on a cross by the very people he has created?

For many people today, Christianity is a curious exercise just as obscure as the game of cricket is to the uninitiated. All that talk about *propitiation*, *reconciliation*, and *salvation* might as well be a foreign language. And what about those strange Scriptures which tell us that in order to live we have to die, that to receive we must give, that to love God we may have to "hate" our own families? In the eyes of many, that makes even less sense than cricket.

So what would it take to persuade the nonbeliever that he or she can really know God? If someone wants to understand the game of cricket, a careful reading of the rule book would be a good start. Similarly, an earnest reading of the Bible would be a good start in coming to know God. But the Bible is hardly meant to be simply a "rule book," despite the large number of people who tend to view it as one. Far surpassing any such comparison, the Bible is meant to reveal to us nothing less than the wonder of God and the mystery of faith!

It seems straightforward enough: "Faith comes from hearing the message, and the message is heard through the word of Christ," Paul told the Romans. If we would just read our Bibles, we would have faith all wrapped up in a neat little package—or so it might seem. But as Paul acknowledged to Timothy, "Beyond all question, the mystery of godliness is great!"

What, for example, explains how two people can read the same Bible, with one turning to God in faith, and the other turning away in doubt and skepticism? What activates the transition between reading or hearing the gospel and actually becoming a person of faith?

Listening to a recent radio interview, I heard a lifelong cricket fan describe what he thought was memorable about the game. I was amazed to hear him say, "Cricket is a contemplative game which has inspired poetry, art, and music." I confess I had never really thought about it that way! But whatever it is about cricket that makes so many people avid fans, you just *know* that there has to be more to it than simply understanding the way the game is played. Surely there is something quite special about the *spirit* of the game!

In that regard, I rather like the old-timer's use of the word *contemplative*. It takes us to an often-overlooked aspect of faith which may actually be the key to the mysterious process of transforming someone who has biblical knowledge into a person with genuine, enthusiastic faith!

When it comes to searching out the wonder of God, none of us wants to be merely a technician. There is so much more to appreciate about our faith, so much more to *feel* and to *be*! What is it that instills the *passion*? What is it about Christian faith that becomes *obsessive*? What is it that would cause a person to *live for its teaching* and *die for its truths*?

If I told you the answer is found in the working of the Holy Spirit, would it seem too simplistic, or perhaps simply too tired and overworn? Does mention of the Holy Spirit sound too mystical to really matter? Have those words *Holy Spirit* become an expression that easily passes across our lips but seems to make little difference when it comes to the crunch?

The Holy Spirit is not a magic wand we wave so that all of a sudden we catch fire in our faith. Nor does the Holy Spirit overwhelm us so as to make all believers supernatural miracle-workers. And you can be sure that being filled with the Spirit won't help any of us find a parking place or "hit for six" in a game of cricket!

What then does the Holy Spirit do to make God come alive in our hearts? He *awakens* us! He *stirs* us! He *enlightens* us!

If faith comes by hearing, and hearing by the Word of God, it is the Holy Spirit who makes sure we actually hear the truths that transform.

As a teacher, I think I recognize something of the role that the Holy Spirit plays in each of our lives. Giving my students reading assignments is only a first step in their learning process. Having been a student myself, I know how easy it is to let one's mind wander, or even to fall asleep, while reading the assigned material. The role of the Holy Spirit is to say, "Wake up and catch what God is saying to you through his Word!" He *awakens* us and *stirs* us to seek God with intensity.

But because knowledge alone is not enough, the Holy Spirit also *enlightens* us, in the manner of a good teacher. As a law professor, I aspire to the thought Jesus expressed when he said, "Therefore every teacher of the law who has been instructed about the kingdom of heaven is like the owner of a house who brings out of his storeroom new treasures as well as old." That is exactly what the Holy Spirit does.

Have you ever read a familiar passage of Scripture—perhaps one you have studied many times through the years—and suddenly get a message that you've never gotten before? Have you ever had the feeling of a light being switched on? "Yes, of course!" you exclaim. "How could I ever have missed seeing that before?"

In your previous readings you may have just tripped over the passage lightly without seeing the obvious, or you may have been looking through the tinted glasses of a particular doctrinal tradition. Or perhaps by now you have simply matured in your overall understanding of God's Word. On the other hand, it may be that the Holy Spirit is *actively reaching out* to make sure that you get the intended message to meet some particular need. The Holy Spirit may well be blessing you with "new treasures" so that the "eyes of your heart may be enlightened."

John Calvin pictured enlightenment as taking place "when the Spirit, with a wondrous and special energy, forms the ear to hear and the mind to understand." It's what the two men on the road to Emmaus described when they finally realized it was the risen Lord with whom they had been talking: "They asked each other, 'Were not our hearts burning within us while he talked with us on the road and opened the Scriptures to us?'"

As Christians, we don't receive some new and private revelation that no one else receives, for through the written Word we already have "the faith that was once for all entrusted to the saints." But the special gift of the Holy Spirit is to give us an openness to *receive* and to *understand* God's revelation for our own individual lives. This is what Jesus did in his post-resurrection appearance to the disciples when he "opened their minds so they could understand the Scriptures."

One of my favorite hymns, written by Charles H. Scott, is a prayer for just such openness and enlightenment:

Open my eyes, that I may see
Glimpses of truth Thou hast for me;
Place in my hands the wonderful key
That shall unclasp, and set me free.

Open my ears, that I may hear
Thy word of truth Thou sendest clear;
And while the wavenotes fall on my ear,
Everything false will disappear.

Silently now I wait for Thee,
Ready, my God, Thy will to see;
Open my eyes, illumine me,
Savior divine!

Illumination! That's what enlightens us. It is what kindles our passion and truly transforms us. For it is when we *really* come to know the God of the Bible that he actually becomes the Lord of our lives! And that is when having God in our lives begins to make a difference.

When we have been enlightened through the Word, God becomes real to us. His love is no longer an abstract concept, but our daily motivation to serve others, as Christ served. To sacrifice for others, as Christ sacrificed. To live morally pure, as Christ was morally pure.

Once enlightened, our faith is no longer simply a matter of trying to follow the rules. Who could ever be passionate about living one's life for a rule book? Cricket fans are not enthusiastic just because they understand the game better than I do. Like all sports fans, they get excited at the prospect of winning. That's even more true of a faith whose God has already been victorious. Once enlightened, faith becomes a matter of *victory*! Victory over sin. Victory over seemingly insurmountable circumstances. Victory even over death!

But the most crucial victory is over our own disbelief. It is at the moment when we cry out "I do believe; help me overcome my unbelief!" that God, working through the Holy Spirit, transforms us from curious spectators into enthusiastic participants. Just exactly how it happens remains a mystery. At one moment our eyes are closed; the next moment they are open. At some point a miracle happens and we believe. Nothing could be more exhilarating than experiencing the enlightenment which comes from a fresh understanding of his Word, with its miraculous power to truly transform!

I only hope that those who stand on the perimeter of my life looking on with curiosity can catch something of the vision and enthusiasm that I have found in Christ. It would be a tragedy if they walked away wondering what could possibly be of value in my Christian faith. But wouldn't it be wonderful to think that the Holy Spirit could use *your* transformed life and *mine* as a means of illuminating their lives as well!

Chapter Twenty-nine

"Along
unfamiliar
paths I will
guide him."

ISAIAH 42:16

EXAMPLE

Signposts

When I first started walking in the Cotswolds, I often found myself lost, confused, and finding myself back where I had been an hour before. It took me some time to find my way around. Along the local footpaths—on gates, posts, trees, and rocks—are yellow arrows pointing the way to the next crossing or turning one must take. And maps and guidebooks are also available to chart one's course o'er hill and dale. But by no means is that the whole story.

Despite the signposts and the maps pointing out specific landmarks, time and nature have a cruel way of hiding the path. All it takes is for summer foliage or a fallen tree to obscure one of those landmarks, and a person can easily become disoriented. As simple as it first sounds, getting from point A to point B can be somewhat mystifying for the novice.

Oh, there is little danger of ever getting seriously lost, since you are never far from civilization in these parts. It's just that searching for hidden or confusing signposts can often be a frustration. Just about the time you give up on following directions and head out on your own, invariably you find yourself facing a definite no-go area defended by threatening strands of rusty barbed wire!

I am happy to report that my days as a novice are over. Now that I've walked these hills for several years, I consider myself somewhat of a veteran. The proper footpaths and the sign-posts which mark them are like old familiar friends. We greet each other almost daily.

Interestingly, my familiarity with the territory usually comes as a surprise to British ramblers. Occasionally I will see people peering intently at their maps and scouring the terrain for those all-important yellow arrows. When I figure they are truly in need of assistance, I try to lend a helping hand. But upon hearing my American accent, many of them skeptically peg me for a wandering tourist out for a stroll in virgin territory. I am the last person they would ever expect to show them the way. Nevertheless, they are grateful. Being able to rely on my experience means they don't have to depend so much on their own reckoning.

Recognizing the difficulty of finding one's way along unfamiliar footpaths makes me appreciate all the more the life of Jesus. Having a personal guide, rather than simply printed guidelines, makes all the difference. You don't have to be in the Cotswolds to appreciate the point. Who wants to read some inscrutable instruction manual when your neighbor is a computer whiz and would be more than happy to sort out that frustrating "error prompt" that keeps flashing on your screen? Given a choice, we would rather go for the personal touch.

In a spiritual sense, it is all the difference between the *written* Word and the *incarnate* Word. When I am in the midst of some important decision or a confusing time in my life, what a tremendous help it is to have some godly friend give me counsel and advice! And in Christ that blessing is multiplied many fold. As the hymn says, What a friend we have in Jesus!

Not that the written Word is unimportant. I agree with Jeremiah's sentiments: that it is not within myself to direct my own steps. I know all too well how terribly lost and confused I get when I impetuously set out on my own! That is why God's revelation is so important to me. Holy Scripture is not just a collection of interesting stories, divine drama, and stirring poetry; Holy Scripture contains all the necessary signposts to point me to God.

Yet even the written Word can have its drawbacks. It's too easy for human tradition to obscure the meaning of the text or for human nature to look for loopholes—those spiritual shortcuts which inevitably take us off the beaten path. Little wonder, then, that God comes to our rescue in the form of a *personal* Guide—the spoken and written Word *made flesh*!

In Jesus we have a reliable guide in whose footsteps we can confidently follow. "Follow my example," Paul told the Corinthians, "as I follow the example of Christ." When Jesus called the chosen Twelve, saying "Follow me," he was also calling us, saying "Follow me, for I am the Way."

If you were to say to me that following Jesus is not always easy, I would have to agree with you. Invariably, he insists on taking me along the highest path—the one that stretches every fiber of my being. Nevertheless, wherever he leads, I know it's the *right* path.

Fortunately, there is more to following Jesus than simply staying on the right path. Through the example laid down by Jesus, abstract biblical precepts are given ultimate personal expression. Faith is no longer a matter of struggling to understand written directions, but a matter of following in the footsteps of the One who has gone before me—in life, in death, and in the life to come.

But here the metaphor must change. No longer are we "following" Jesus—as if separated by some distance—but we have

Christ *in* us, bringing life, and strength, and hope. With Christ *in* us, never is the destination clearer!

How very odd it is that more people don't want to follow Jesus and have him intimately involved in their lives. I can guarantee you that, despite my American accent, I've never had anyone who was lost on the local footpaths turn down my offer to help them find the way. It's all the more intriguing why those who were spiritually lost on the backroads of Judea in the first century would reject Jesus simply because he didn't fit their preconceived idea of a spiritual leader.

Why is it, then, that more people don't want to follow Jesus and allow him intimate access to their lives? Is it a matter of stubborn pride? Is it a matter of misplaced trust in their own spiritual insight? Or is it just possible that they are actually convinced they aren't lost in the first place?

Some years ago, evangelistic believers attempted to capture the attention of a nonbelieving world by displaying bumper stickers which read: "I've found it!" The idea was to generate enough curiosity for nonbelievers to ask what the person had found, and thus to create an opportunity for sharing one's faith.

It wasn't long before skeptics responded with their own bumper stickers, haughtily declaring, "I never lost it!" How is anyone ever going to help others find their way spiritually if they don't even recognize how hopelessly lost they are?

But here is where we ourselves have to be careful. Maybe it's obvious, but if we are in any way to lead the spiritually lost, we know that we mustn't end up *following them instead.* There's no denying that the way of the world is enticing and seductive. If we're not careful, just about the time we think we're the ones doing the leading, we could easily wake up and realize that we're the ones doing the following! And if we're following *them* instead of going in another direction, they could be excused for thinking that they are on the right path.

True leadership begins by being genuinely different in the eyes of the world. Only the most obstinate person sees someone going along in a different direction without at least making a mental note that a different path does in fact exist. And who knows—many of the more curious seekers might even wonder if it is a *better* path.

That's when it becomes important for me to be more than a map reader for myself—or a map interpreter for others, for that matter. If someone sees me crossing a field in a direction he has never considered before, it is *me* he is watching—not a map.

In terms of spiritual guidance, these are people who may never have read the Bible for themselves, or people who have read it but can't seem to make sense of it. It is in our daily walk among friends, loved ones, and business associates that you and I become the "letters known and read by everybody." Whether or not we think of ourselves as spiritual leaders, the truth is that, day by day, we are leading people either *to* or *away from* a relationship with God.

For many onlookers I am a human signpost—a yellow arrow on the road of life that points them down one path or another. And it is here—right here—that it makes such a crucial difference whether or not I have made the transition from simply "following" Christ at a distance to actually having Christ *in* me. Is Christ really at the center of my life? Have I been transformed by his strength and power? Does my relationship with Christ make a difference, moment by moment, in what direction I take?

Considering the spiritual consequences which other people potentially face, I've got to answer a no-holds-barred question about myself: If people follow my example, will I be leading them in the right direction?

Chapter Thirty

"Serve the Lord your
God with all your heart
and with all your soul."

Deuteronomy 10:12

COMMITMENT

Nettles

W arning! Not all the English countryside is cozy, charming, friendly, and inviting. On my walks I've been pricked, stung, scratched, and even cut. For every lovely flower, tree, or shrub there is a painfully aggressive thistle, thorny vine, or nettle just waiting in ambush. Of them all, I think the innocent-looking nettle is the nastiest. Thistles and thorny vines are sufficiently recognizable that normally I am able to avoid them. But nettles look like any other harmless green plant—until it's too late!

Ever heard the expression "grasping the nettle"? Each time I pass by a particular area of nettles at the edge of the chestnut coppice, I'm tempted to try it. Just *tempted*, you understand— I've never really done it. But if I knew it would really work, I would do it. In fact, I keep thinking how neat it would be actually to have done it—actually to have "grasped the nettle"!

Even my wavering about whether to try doing it proves the whole point of the exercise. The expression comes from those times when a person needs to make a crucial decision which is thrust upon him by adverse circumstances. Given those difficult circumstances, it is said that a person needs to "grasp the nettle" and get on with it. It's all about having the courage and boldness to do the right thing even if it appears costly. Unlike my abstract desire to test the theory, the phrase itself is typically associated with some great uninvited risk.

Also inherent within the expression is the suggestion that *grasping* the nettle—quickly, firmly, and with confidence—will prevent the painful prickly sensation you get from tentatively touching the nettle. That a nettle is less likely to sting when it is grasped firmly is the point of these lines, written by Aaron Hill (1685-1750):

> *Tender-handed stroke a nettle,*
> *And it stings you for your pains;*
> *Grasp it like a man of mettle,*
> *And it soft as silk remains.*

I can vouch for the stinging pain that courses through the body when my hand accidentally comes into contact with the menacing hairs on the nettle's leaves. The pain is not the simple pricking of the thistle, which seemingly derives pleasure out of hearing a person gasp, but is then content to run away. No, nettles insist on lingering pain and prolonged suffering. With nettles, I always feel as if I've been shot with a poison arrow, and the throbbing can last for hours.

Little wonder that I'm so hesitant to test the poem's theory about the absence of pain where one quickly and decidedly *grasps* a nettle! Since I know exactly what it's going to feel like if I'm wrong, I'm not willing to take the risk. Mere curiosity is hardly a sufficient motivation, given the risk of pain and the almost useless value of knowing for certain whether it really works.

It seems to me that my dilemma about "grasping the nettle" is somewhat like the hesitancy with which most of us approach surrender to God. Casual contact with some kind of faith would be nice to experience if it weren't for the demands that faith makes in return. To many people, having faith in God appears onerous and burdensome. It means giving up a particular pleasure or making some other far-more-significant lifestyle change. Can knowing God be worth the sacrifice?

Many of us have walked with God for a long time, and it's a comfortable feeling. Church on Sundays, perhaps a Bible study during the week, and we're in. As long as we keep our noses clean, the rest of the time we can live pretty much the same as everybody else.

But Jesus doesn't seem to leave much room for half-hearted discipleship. It sounds as if I must either surrender to him *all the way* or just quit pretending: "He who is not with me is against me." Emblazoned on my mind is that scathing rebuke of the believers in Laodicea: "I know your deeds, that you are neither cold nor hot. I wish you were either one or the other! So, because you are *lukewarm*—neither hot nor cold—I am about to spit you out of my mouth."

Can we really work both sides of the street? Can we really hold onto God with one hand and onto the world with the other? It was Jesus who said, "No one can serve two masters." And it was Joshua who said, "Choose for yourselves this day whom you will serve!"

Most of us flounder about, *wanting* to be fully committed followers of Jesus—*thinking* about it, coming *close*—yet never quite getting to the point where we are willing to "grasp the nettle"—to give ourselves *wholly* to God. To empty ourselves *totally* of self-will and self-direction. To surrender *completely* to Christ.

We all fear the unknown. What would my life be like if I *really* gave my life over to God? What would my family think of me? How would it affect my job or career? What would it cost me financially? With all that at risk, do I really want to "grasp the nettle" of full surrender?

The rich young man who asked Jesus what he needed to do to inherit eternal life was probably taken by surprise when Jesus said, "One thing you lack....Go, sell everything you have and give to the poor, and you will have treasure in heaven." The young man had taken great pride and comfort in having strictly obeyed the commandments (which he could do without any terribly great sacrifice). But asking him to give up his possessions in order to have eternal life was too much to ask.

I suspect that Jesus looked deeper than the young man's unwillingness to sell his possessions. It wasn't a rich man giving away all his money that mattered to Jesus. What Jesus undoubtedly saw was a heart that was unwilling to completely surrender to God. Whether possessions, career, or perhaps some relationship, something would always stand in his way. But for the *fully surrendered* heart, no sacrifice is too great.

The story of the rich young man makes us think about our own willingness to surrender. What "treasures" in our own lives are we unwilling to give up for God? Is there something we feel we must hold onto at all cost?

Surrendering to God is the most difficult decision we will ever make. The prophet Joel reminds us that we are not alone when we face the moment of choosing: "Multitudes, multitudes in the valley of decision! For the day of the Lord is near in the valley of decision." What Joel really means is that most of us live an entire lifetime in the valley of *indecision*. To surrender or not to surrender—*that* is the ultimate question of life!

It was the prophet Elijah—not in a valley, but on a mountaintop—who cautioned us that we can't keep putting off that decision forever. Remember his contest with the prophets of Baal? "Elijah went before the people and said, 'How long will you waver between two opinions? If the Lord is God, follow him; but if Baal is God, follow him.' But the people said nothing."

Saying *nothing* is saying *everything*! Wavering and waffling are hardly the characteristics of a life fully turned over to God. On-again-off-again commitment is simply a red flag signaling that we have yet to give up self and trust completely in God's leading.

Joshua had no doubts about surrendering his life to God: "As for me and my household, we will serve the Lord." Despite the risk, Joshua? Despite the cost? For Joshua, the greater risks and greater costs lay in the alternative to surrender. It was not merely a matter of jeopardizing one's lifestyle, or ego, or bank account. For Joshua, surrender to God was nothing less than a matter of life and death.

Speaking to the people of Israel, it was Moses who had put those choices in stark perspective: "This day I call heaven and earth as witnesses against you that I have set before you life and death, blessings and curses. Now choose life, so that you and your children may live and that you may love the Lord your God, listen to his voice, and hold fast to him. For the Lord is your life...."

As long as you're grasping, says Moses, make sure that what you grasp is *life*, not death. Grasping for self-direction is grasping only at straws; it misses the true meaning of life: "Whoever loses his life for my sake will find it."

Never has surrender to God come at greater cost or brought life and death more into perspective than when Jesus confronted the agony of surrender in the Garden of Gethsemane. "Father, if you are willing, take this cup from me," Jesus prayed with such intensity that he sweat drops of blood. "Yet not my will, but yours be done," he whispered in final full surrender.

Unlike the rich young man, Jesus had no possessions to give up. At that point, the only thing Jesus had that he could possibly surrender to God was his life. But for him who showed us the path to complete surrender, not even death was too great a cost. For Jesus knew what we tend to forget: that surrender doesn't lead to death, but to life; that there is freedom in submission, and liberation in wholehearted, unwavering commitment!

"Grasping the nettle." No one has ever done it like Jesus. "Not my will, but yours!" Can we even *begin* to say that? If not, "Let us fix our eyes on Jesus, the author and perfecter of our faith, who for the joy set before him endured the cross, scorning its shame, and sat down at the right hand of the throne of God."

Then with Paul we will be able to say, "I have been crucified with Christ and I no longer live, but Christ lives in me. The life I live in the body, I live by faith in the Son of God, who loved me and gave himself for me."

Through his complete surrender on the cross, Jesus has already grasped the nettle for us. He has taken away the sting of death. All we need to do is to put our hand in his—to feel the softness of his love and never let go!

Chapter Thirty-one

"Play the harp well,
sing many a song,
so that you will
be remembered."

Isaiah 23:16

SIGNIFICANCE

Gravestones

Each week, organized groups of ramblers regularly make their way across the hills in this part of the Cotswolds. Six, twelve, even two dozen at a time. In wave after wave they come. From wherever throughout Britain they may have started their journey, they are dropped off on the Stow Road near the village of Stanway, home to Lord Niepath's stately old manor. From Stanway, the ramblers make their way on the lower path through Stanton, Laverton, and finally alongside my cottage in Buckland.

Oftentimes, organized groups stop for lunch at the long house overlooking the fish ponds at the top of the village. Their cheery hostess, Margaret Birt, will have prepared a sumptuous home-cooked buffet which is served right in the middle of her country kitchen. Reluctantly tearing themselves away from the table, they then trek on across the top of Burhill and down into Broadway, where they are picked up and carried home, exhausted but exhilarated.

I'm often curious what they think about as they walk through Stanton, particularly as they are leaving the village. There the walking path leads from the commemorative cross

on the main road, down the lane to the church; then diago-
nally through the churchyard, and beside a long, high stone
wall before disgorging its wandering guests into the fields
beyond. Do those who walk this way take any notice of the
history beneath their feet? Do they stop to consider the faded
aspirations and discarded status of those whose spent lives quietly rustle beneath their pounding footsteps?

As with most churchyards in England, the ground there
is blanketed by ancient gravestones. Weatherworn and precariously tilting at odd angles, some of the old slates date
back to the 1700s. A few of the gravestones tell interesting
short stories about loved ones, as seen through the loving
eye of memory by those who survived. One of the most
unusual and poignant inscriptions is found on a stone
located on the west side of the church in the direction of
the manor house:

Elizabeth Lee
1877-1960
Beloved nanny to three generations

Suffer little children to come unto me
And forbid them not, for of such is the
kingdom of heaven

I can only imagine a woman who, although she never married, was a mother to many, a woman of love and strength
whose influence lives on today in the lives of those whose care
was entrusted to her.

Unfortunately, many of the gravestones have been worn by
time so that the names of those who are buried beneath them
are unreadable. Mute, moss-covered monuments, they are like
silent sentries guarding the secret identity of the departed.

Who were these people who lived and died hundreds of years
ago? They might have been butchers, bakers, and candlestick

makers, but the mere fact that they have impressive gravestones raises the odds that they were people of position in their day. Past Lords of the Manor, perhaps, or vicars, or successful barristers. Few nannies would have been honored like Elizabeth Lee.

The people of position, like such people today, must have gone about their lives accomplishing what seemed at the time to be important, even invaluable, tasks. The little people around them must have bowed and scraped at their every command, for that is how it was in a society scrupulously separated by classes.

But today, whether master or servant, they all lie side by side beneath the sod—some with gravestones, others lying in the same anonymity with which they lived out their entire lives. In the end, did it matter that one was a master and the other a servant? Today, chattering ramblers with backpacks and boots walk briskly over their remains, oblivious to the "important, even invaluable tasks" that were achieved in days gone by.

When I walk through these same gravestones, I can't help but think of Solomon's words: "Generations come and generations go, but the earth remains forever....There is no remembrance of men of old, and even those who are yet to come will not be remembered by those who follow." No wonder Solomon was tempted to conclude that life—at least as we live it—is meaningless!

As the world's wisest man, Solomon gives me little comfort in the thought that, no matter how special I might think I am, in generations to come no one will care. "For the wise man, like the fool, will not be long remembered; in days to come both will be forgotten. Like the fool, the wise man too must die!" Deep down I know Solomon is right about that, despite the irony that he himself has proved to be a notable exception to the rule.

Yet does the fact that you and I might not be remembered a century from now really bother us? For myself, I have lived a full life and look forward with anticipation to an even fuller life hereafter. However, what I do wonder about is whether the living of my life will have made any difference. I suppose that family and friends would be kind enough to say that I had "touched their lives" while in their midst, but the same would be true of every individual who ever lived. Others are always affected, for good or for ill.

No, the question is whether there is any *significant* way in which I have touched the lives of others. Or as it is sometimes put, Is the world better off for my having been here? What will be my legacy to future generations? Surely we've all wondered whether life will have any lasting meaning beyond our death. Perhaps the secret lies in thinking back on the significance of others who, by their simple acts of devotion or their desire for excellence, have helped us to dream big dreams and challenged us to reach beyond ourselves.

When fears of eventual insignificance sweep over me, I always think of my high school English teacher, Sally R. Wilson. It was Sally who taught me to write. Without her, who knows whether any of the words in my books ever would have surfaced to really make a difference in anyone's life. If the thoughts are mine, the words are Sally's. In case she ever wondered, her life was not without significance. It led to changed lives.

I think the same must be true of Sally's mother—a woman whom I never met, and whose name I never heard. Given the typical circumstances of her generation, however, I suspect that Sally's mother was "just a housewife," probably with ten children to raise as best she could in hard times. Undoubtedly, she too must have considered whether her obscure life would matter on the grand scale of things. But if it hadn't been for the sacrifices she made for Sally—and probably the proud encouragement she gave to Sally's education—I might never have sat at Sally's feet.

If the words in my books are Sally's, the love that gave them to Sally came from her mother. Her life was not without significance. It led to changed lives.

Changed lives—that's what is ultimately important for each of us. That's what will truly last. The greatest good we may ever accomplish may be through someone else whose life we have influenced in seemingly insignificant ways. Take Peter, for example. We remember Peter as the one who preached so powerfully to the crowds gathered on Pentecost and who gave his life in sacrificial service to the early church. But do we remember his brother Andrew, who first told Peter about the Messiah? What a difference Andrew made in the life of Peter, and through Peter, in the lives of countless thousands, including ourselves!

And how could we forget the young evangelist, Timothy, who was so instrumental in the spread of the gospel? But do we remember that his faith "first lived in his grandmother Lois and in his mother Eunice"? Whether it was Lois, or Eunice, or Sally Wilson's mother—or even Elizabeth Lee with no children of her own—we are reminded of what a powerful influence for good lies in the godly hand that rocks the cradle. There is no greater significance in all the world—whether for a father or a mother—than bringing up children "in the training and instruction of the Lord."

Changed lives are our greatest legacy. Changed lives are the gifts that truly keep on giving, generation after generation. No matter how seemingly insignificant our own lives, we achieve significance through the lives that we touch for good. And never are our lives more significant than when the lives we touch are brought to know Christ. For at that point lives are not simply changed, but *transformed!*

As you look back, who are those who have significantly touched your life at some point along the way? If it's still possible, today might be a good day to let them know how much you appreciate it. And if you've ever wondered about your own significance, just look around you. Think of all the lives you are changing, or *could* change, even today.

Whether what I do is seen in the eyes of the world to be great or small, I only ask that when future generations pass unknowingly by my weathered gravestone, someone might be walking on a different path because of something I have done. And not just a *different* path, but a *higher* one.

Scripture References

In Quiet Places
Genesis 5:24; 6:9; Micah 6:8

1. *Rabbits*—
Matthew 13:9,13-15; John 8:47; 1 Kings 19:12

2. *Balloons*—
John 20:29; Romans 6:22; 8:1,2; John 8:32-36

3. *Graffiti*—
Psalm 69:4; Acts 13:22; Psalm 69:7; 64:1-4; 35:15,24,25; 55:12-14,20-21; 1 Samuel 19:9,10; 2 Samuel 15:1-12; Psalm 41:9; 69:24,27,28; 109:8-12; 1 Peter 4:8; Proverbs 10:12; Psalm 23:5,6; Luke 23:34,46; Psalm 31:5

4. *Church Bells*—
Exodus 28:31-36; Zechariah 14:20; John 17:19; Matthew 27:51; Hebrews 10:19-22; 4:14-16

5. *The Old Church Wall*—
John 5:1-8; Matthew 15:21-28; Luke 19:2-10; 18:16; John 8:3-11; Luke 7:36-50

6. *Snowfall*—
Psalm 51:7; 1-3; Isaiah 1:18; Luke 3:5,6; Psalm 23:1; Lamentations 3:23

7. *Jacob Sheep*—
Genesis 30:25–31:13; Matthew 5:28,29; 6:22,23; Proverbs 4:23; Psalm 105:4; 1 John 3:2,3; Philippians 4:8; James 3:11,12

8. *Warplanes*—
Job 1:13-19; James 4:1; Matthew 4:1-11; Mark 1:35; 14:32; Ephesians 6:11-17; Luke 2:14

9. *Jumbo the Elephant*—
John 6:5-15; Mark 10:35-40; 1 Corinthians 1:23-28; Matthew 5:1-12; 19:30; Luke 9:48; Matthew 10:39; 27:41-44

10. *Seasons*—
Acts 14:17; Genesis 1:14; Psalm 74:17; Jeremiah 8:7; Ecclesiastes 3:1-8; Psalm 30:5; Lamentations 3:23; Hebrews 11:11; Hosea 14:8; Exodus 2:23,24; 2 Timothy 2:13; Isaiah 51:11; Psalm 137:1,4; Deuteronomy 7:9; Hebrews 13:8

11. *Dream House*—
Ecclesiastes 5:10; Luke 12:15-21; Philippians 4:12; 1 Timothy 6:6,7; Colossians 3:2

12. *The Badger*—
Genesis 1:26-28; 9:1-3; Deuteronomy 25:4; 22:6,7; Colossians 3:12; 2 Peter 1:5-7; Galatians 5:22,23; Hosea 11:3,4; 1 John 4:19; Luke 22:61,62; Matthew 7:12; 19:19

13. *Walking Stick*—
Zechariah 8:4; Psalm 23; 1 Samuel 15:3; Ephesians 1:17-21; Romans 8:37-39; Philippians 4:13; John 15:15

14. *Lambing Time*—
John 10:2-4; 10:14,15; 10:5; 1 Corinthians 2:14; 1 John 4:1

15. *The Rectory*—
Matthew 23:27; Ecclesiastes 12:8; 3:20; 9:9; 12:1; Ephesians 2:10; Ecclesiastes 12:7; 12:5; 1 Corinthians 15:55; Ecclesiastes 12:13,14; Matthew 23:38; Galatians 3:27

16. *Gates*—
Revelation 21:21; John 10:9; Matthew 11:28; Revelation 22:17; John 10:1,9,10; 14:6; Luke 15:11-32; John 14:2; 1 Corinthians 2:9; Isaiah 64:4; Revelation 21:1-5; 1 Corinthians 2:10

17. *The Sheep*—
Genesis 1:26,27; 2:19,20; 2:23; 1 John 3:11; Matthew 19:19; 5:44; John 1:29,36; Luke 6:35; Matthew 5:44-46; Luke 23:34

18. *Darkness*—
Psalm 119:104,105; 27:1; 23:4; 139:11,12; Genesis 1:3; John 8:12

19. *Holiday Cottages*—
Genesis 2:3; Deuteronomy 5:12-15; Mark 16:2; Acts 20:7; 1 Corinthians 16:2; Mark 6:31,32

20. *Exercise*—
Psalm 121:1; 1 Corinthians 9:25; 1 Timothy 4:8; Ecclesiastes 12:12; 1:13; Proverbs 2:1-5; Habakkuk 3:19; Isaiah 40:29-31; Exodus 15:2; Psalm 84:5-7; Joshua 14:10,11; Judges 16:17; 2 Samuel 22:30,33; Matthew 19:26; Philippians 4:13; Proverbs 31:25

21. *Sheep Droppings*—
Matthew 25:14-30; Exodus 17:12; 1 Corinthians 12:17-19,22-24; Matthew 19:30; Esther 4:14; Ecclesiastes 12:13

22. *The Cemetery*—
Romans 6:3,4; Luke 22:19,20; 1 Corinthians 11:26; Philippians 1:21; Ecclesiastes 3:11; Psalm 90:12

23. *The Hunt*—
Ecclesiastes 4:6; Matthew 6:19; 6:31-33

24. *Five Black Cows—*
James 5:14-16; 2 Corinthians 1:3-5; Psalm 103:13; Isaiah 49:13,15; Job 2:11; John 11:19; Isaiah 40:1

25. *Gargoyles—*
Isaiah 2:6; Genesis 31:30-35; Exodus 32:1-35; Isaiah 44:14,16-20; Psalm 135:16-18; 91:1-6; Deuteronomy 28:52; Isaiah 31:1

26. *The Greenhouse—*
Romans 7:22,23; 7:15,18; 6:1,2; 1 Corinthians 13:11,12; John 3:6; 6:63; Romans 8:11

27. *Sunsets—*
Psalm 85:10,11; 1 Corinthians 1:9; John 3:16; Luke 2:14; Ephesians 2:14; Colossians 1:19,20; John 16:33; Romans 5:1,2; Isaiah 60:20

28. *Cricket—*
Matthew 10:39; Acts 20:35; Matthew 10:37; Romans 10:17; 1 Timothy 3:16; Matthew 13:52; Ephesians 1:18; Luke 24:32; Jude 3; Luke 24:45; Mark 9:24

29. *Signposts—*
Jeremiah 10:23; 1 Corinthians 11:1; Matthew 4:19; John 14:6; Galatians 2:20; Mark 6:1-3; 2 Corinthians 3:2

30. *Nettles—*
Matthew 12:30; Revelation 3:15,16; Matthew 6:24; Joshua 24:15; Mark 10:21; Joel 3:14; 1 Kings 18:21; Deuteronomy 30:19,20; Matthew 10:39; Luke 22:42; Hebrews 12:2; Galatians 2:20

31. *Gravestones—*
Ecclesiastes 1:4,11; 2:17; 2:16; John 1:35-41; 2 Timothy 1:5; Ephesians 6:4

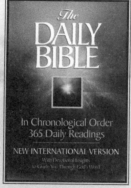

The Daily Bible
In Chronological Order; 365 Daily Readings
by F. LaGard Smith

Get caught in the excitement of God's unfolding plan!

In this dynamic and refreshing Scripture narrative, you'll discover biblical events in the order they occurred. The *Daily Bible* features:

- ✣ a chronological/historical arrangement of every Bible book
- ✣ 365 convenient daily reading segments
- ✣ the New International Version text
- ✣ topical arrangements for Proverbs and Ecclesiastes
- ✣ insightful devotional commentary

As you experience the sweep of biblical history, you'll gain a cohesive understanding of biblical times and a greater appreciation for God's constant provision and loving interactions with His people.